Praise for *Confessions of a Credit Junkie*

"Imagine having someone who actually reads the fine print in credit card offers and guides you through the perks—and the traps. That expert is Beverly Harzog, and her story will both entertain and educate you. She knows what she's talking about when it comes to credit cards, and she loves to share that knowledge. When it comes to credit and debt, listen to what she has to say. Her advice, as they say, is priceless."

—Gerri Detweiler, host of Talk Credit Radio, author and director of consumer education for Credit.com

Confessions of a Credit Junkie

Everything You Need to Know to Avoid the Mistakes I Made

Beverly Harzog

CAREER
PRESS

The Career Press, Inc.
Pompton Plains, NJ

CONFESSIONS OF A CREDIT JUNKIE
EDITED BY ROGER SHEETY
Cover design by Amanda Kain
Printed in the U.S.A.

To order this title, please call toll-free 1-800-CAREER-1 (NJ and Canada: 201-848-0310) to order using VISA or MasterCard, or for further information on books from Career Press.

The Career Press, Inc.
220 West Parkway, Unit 12
Pompton Plains, NJ 07444
www.careerpress.com

Library of Congress Cataloging-in-Publication Data
CIP Data Available Upon Request.

This book is dedicated to my husband, Bernd, and my two terrific kids, Ashley and Grant. I couldn't have done this without your love and support.

Acknowledgments

Playing on the theme of this book, I'll make a confession. The only time I ever read the Acknowledgments in books was when I was looking for an agent.

That was a long time ago because I've been with my agent, Marilyn Allen, for years now. I owe a world of gratitude to her. Thank you, Marilyn, for believing in this project and never giving up on it. You're the best agent ever! I'd also like to thank my editor, Roger Sheety. You were a pleasure to work with!

I can't thank my family enough for being supportive no matter how cranky I got from the long hours of writing. We got Marshall, an 8-week-old Maltese puppy, a week before I signed the contract for this book. Thank you to my husband, Bernd, and my kids, Ashley and Grant, for doing more than your share of the puppy-raising duties so I could keep on writing. I'm so blessed to have such a loving and giving family.

I'm so honored that Liz Weston wrote the Foreword for this book. Thank you, Liz, for your generosity. You have helped so many people with your advice. You are a personal finance rock star! I'd like to thank Gerri Detweiler. Gerri, when I first started working at Credit.com, you became my instant friend. I'm very grateful to you for all the times you shared your media tips and credit expertise with me. I still miss working with you! And I also need to thank Adam Levin, the co-founder of Credit.com. You've been a wonderful mentor to me and I appreciate all of your sage advice. I admire you a great deal!

One of my favorite movies of all time is *It's a Wonderful Life*. I love the scene where George Bailey's friends show up and prove that he's wealthy when it comes to friendships. I'm extremely wealthy in this area, and I need to thank a bunch of people for cheering me on and being patient with me when I disappeared for weeks on end.

Thanks to Gina Roberts-Grey, Rosie Russell, Mary Ann Campbell, Kerri Fivecoat-Campbell, and Linda Melone for your emotional support and friendship.

Contents

Foreword by Liz Weston
11

Introduction
15

Chapter 1: 10 Mistakes I Made That You Never Have To
19

Chapter 2: Your Credit Life Explained in Simple Language
35

Chapter 3: What's Your Credit Card Personality?
61

Chapter 4: The Fine Print Made Easy
79

Chapter 5: Your First Credit Card: Build Credit, Stay Debt-Free
95

Chapter 6: Plain Vanilla Credit Cards
109

Chapter 7: Rewards Credit Cards for Fun and Profit
121

Chapter 8: The Good and the Bad of Business Cards
143

Chapter 9: Get Out of Debt With a Balance Transfer Card
159

Chapter 10: Seven Ways to Use a Credit Card to Rebuild Credit
173

Chapter 11: Extreme Credit: Strategies for the Power User
183

Chapter 12: Hot Credit Card Trends to Watch
193

Appendix: A Credit Card Glossary
205

Index
213

About the Author
219

Foreword

Increasingly, young people are turning away from credit cards. That's not necessarily a good thing.

Twice as many people aged 18 to 35 reported having no credit cards in 2012, according to a Mercator Advisory Group study, compared to five years earlier. Those who had cards were less likely to use them for online purchases or to participate in rewards programs.

A similar study conducted by an analyst for Fair Isaac Corp., creators of the leading FICO score, found young people had dramatically reduced the average amount of credit card debt they carried in the same time period. The average debt near the end of 2012 was $2,087, compared to $3,037 five years earlier.

Less credit card debt is wonderful. Eschewing cards entirely, though, isn't necessarily smart.

The responsible use of credit cards—including paying balances in full every month—can help young people build the credit scores they'll need to get good mortgage rates when they're ready to buy homes. Good credit can make it easier to get an apartment in the meantime and win lower rates on their auto insurance. For better or worse, credit scoring has become an influential if not essential part of our finances in the 21st century.

Credit cards also provide important consumer protections, providing a middleman in disputes and keeping fraudsters away from your bank account.

Then there are rewards programs. Savvy deployment of credit cards can reap cash-back rebates, free travel, and other goodies that can be worth hundreds, and sometimes thousands, of dollars each year.

Millions of people use credit cards responsibly every day. More than 35 million households in the United States are in the habit of paying their balances in full. They reap protections and rewards without paying a dime of interest to lenders.

These people are a stark rebuttal against those who assert that credit cards are evil, or that people who stumble into debt can never again trust themselves with plastic.

Beverly Harzog's personal story is an excellent example of how someone can bounce back from early mistakes. Even though she was good with numbers and would become a CPA, Harzog racked up so much credit card debt in her 20s that she eventually couldn't pay her bills. Like many in her situation, she ignored her mail, dodged collectors' calls, and had no idea how deep a hole she'd dug for herself.

Harzog hit bottom when the department store that granted her first-ever card summarily canceled her account. The story of how she bounced back—the story of this book—is a must-read for anyone facing similar troubles, or who wants to avoid the mistakes she made.

Once you're using credit responsibly, Harzog can help you step up your game. Her advice about getting and deploying cards will help you use them to your advantage, rather than letting card issuers take advantage of you.

Confessions of a Credit Junkie makes it clear that credit cards are a tool, part of the financial kit you need in the modern world. Let Beverly Harzog show you how to use this tool to help you build a sound financial future.

Liz Weston,
MSN Money personal finance columnist and
author of the national best-seller *Your Credit Score*

Introduction

For the longest time, I wouldn't talk about my sordid credit card past. After a while, I actually think I managed to wipe it from my memory. No small feat, considering I talk about credit cards every day of the week.

One day, however, I watched a movie that brought back my past in vivid detail. I wish I could say it was a profound movie that exposed corruption or tried to solve world hunger. But it wasn't. It was this unassuming chick flick: *Confessions of a Shopaholic*.

In the summer of 2011, my then-20-year-old daughter, Ashley, asked me if I wanted to watch that movie with her. I jumped at the chance, even though I'd barely heard of it. When your college-student kid wants to spend time with you, you don't ask questions: you just do it. So I told her to pick the time and I'd be there.

If you haven't seen this film, don't worry: I can paint a clear picture of it for you. The movie's heroine, Becky Bloomwood, is a shopaholic who is up to her eyeballs in credit card debt.

Becky can't pay her credit card bills, so she's in that special place I like to call Credit Card Hell. She's getting threatening phone calls from a creepy debt collector. She's afraid to open her mail and look at her credit card statements. And to the audience's delight, Becky's a finance journalist. The irony makes it all the more entertaining.

The beginning of the movie shows a very young Becky, watching tall, beautiful women buying designer goodies with the swipe of a card. She thought these women had "magic cards" that let them walk out of the store with a full shopping bag. With magic cards, you don't need money!

It's funny stuff, right? During the first 30 minutes, Ashley and I were both laughing at Becky's debt dilemma. It was wildly funny right up until the time she started getting calls from a debt collector.

That's when it hit me like a bolt of lightening. Suddenly, my brain was flooded with memories of calls from—not one—*several* debt collectors. I had visions of overstuffed shopping bags, dodging phone calls, and then, when my credit ride came to a merciful end, eating peanut butter and jelly sandwiches for dinner every night so I could pay my bills. The movie was no longer funny because I suddenly realized that a few decades ago, I *was* Becky Bloomwood.

But I wasn't just a financial journalist who couldn't resist a sale on boots. I kicked it up a couple of notches. For one thing, I usually paid full price. I also worked in corporate finance and even became a CPA in the middle of my credit card disaster years. I could calculate earnings per share for a corporate income statement, but I didn't know what my credit score was. Correction: I didn't know I *had* a credit score.

Looking back, it wasn't so much that I was greedy, but truly illiterate when it came to personal finance. Okay, I admit to being a bit greedy. I'd never had money before and I was almost giddy from my sudden paycheck power.

Fast forward about seven years and I was in credit card debt. To this day, I don't know the exact amount of my debt. I think I was worried I'd have a panic attack if I saw the actual number. So when I finally took responsibility and started tackling my debt, I only looked at the minimum payment due and avoided the rest of the statement.

Listen, I don't recommend my crazy approach to debt reduction. It's amazing that I actually succeeded doing it this way. But I was young and self-supporting and scared senseless. So I handled it the best way I knew how under the circumstances. When I finally looked at my debt a year later, I still owed $11,000. So I know my debt was around $20,000 when I started chipping away at it.

It took me two years to get totally out of debt. During this time, I read everything I could find about credit and personal finance. I became so enamored of it that I left my corporate job to become a finance writer. I ended up specializing in credit cards because I wanted to help others avoid the huge mistakes I'd made.

After we finished watching *Confessions of a Shopaholic* that day, I told my daughter everything about my credit card past. I wanted her to know that credit wasn't evil. It's not understanding how credit works that can make it dangerous. I'm the one who got myself in trouble because I didn't learn the rules first.

A few months after watching *Confessions of a Shopaholic*, I toyed with the idea of writing about my credit card past in all its vivid glory. But the thought of that was scary. I really experienced a lot of internal conflict over this. Should I talk about something so personal? Will consumers think less of me? I'm supposed to be an expert, for crying out loud.

And then I thought about the personal finance blogging community. These bloggers put their stories out there every day and I could see from the reader comments that they were helping people by sharing their stories. So I took the plunge and went public, which was not easy for me at all.

I wrote an essay called "Confessions of a Former Credit Card-a-Holic" for Credit.com. My only goal at the time was to let people know that I had made mistakes and that I survived it. I wanted to give people hope that they could not only survive it, but come out on top in the end.

The essay was picked up by MSN Money and The Consumerist, so it got a lot of exposure. When I started getting heartfelt e-mails from people who had read my essay, I knew I'd done the right thing. The common thread in the e-mails was that they felt less alone and less "like a loser" because I'd gone public with this.

Once I started my credit card blog and got in the trenches with consumers, I realized that there was a real need for basic credit card information. Not just to help people stay out of trouble, but also to help them learn how to profit from their credit cards. That's when I got the idea to turn my credit card disaster story into this book.

By the time you finish my book, you'll know how to take advantage of your credit cards so you can take free trips and save a ton on everyday expenses. You'll understand how credit scores work and what's on your credit report. If you're in debt, you'll learn seven simple credit rebuilding strategies. And you'll find out that the fine print isn't scary when you need know how to decipher it. You'll even take a fun quiz to determine your credit card personality. Are you ready? Let's do this thing!

1

10 Mistakes I Made That You Never Have To

You can think of this chapter as the credit card version of the reality TV show *What Not to Wear*. It's an appropriate way to look at it because a lot of my debt came from purchasing designer clothes.

I had a difficult time trying to decide which mistake to talk about first because, you know, they're all pretty big. But when I think back to when it all began, it's really the credit card offers that stick out in my mind.

I know that it seems like a fairly unimportant detail to settle on. But I still remember holding the offer letters and thinking about how important I'd become. It was like a Sally Field moment: You like me! You *really* like me. It didn't cross my mind that millions of other people got these same offers. Basically, the banks *really* liked everyone.

So after I settled on the credit card offers as the first mistake, I started listing all of the other mistakes I made. And, you know what, they kind of fell into a logical progression.

Mistake #1: Applying for every credit card offer

When I was in college, I had only one credit card and that was my Rich's card. In case you've never heard of Rich's, it was a famous department store that was later bought by Macy's in 2005. Rich's was my favorite store because it had a great petite section. I applied for their credit card and I got approved. I didn't have any credit history other than a car loan for a small amount. But even back then, retail cards were pretty easy to get.

When I graduated from college with an accounting degree, I went to work for a petroleum company. The salary was very good. It was to me, anyway, because I'd never had that much money before. Every night when I'd go home after work, I'd check my mailbox. And you wouldn't believe the offers! The envelopes alone were gratifying to read: *You've been pre-selected! You've earned it! You deserve this card!*

I bought into the hype and began to think that, yes, by golly, I did deserve these cards. When I received the first one, from Citi, it was such a rush to pull this shiny card from the envelope and see my name in embossed letters.

And, like most junkies, I wanted to experience that feeling again. And again and again. I applied for several cards all within a few weeks. Keep in mind that this was before the Internet. If the Internet had been available, heaven only knows how many credit cards I would've applied for.

By the time I was done credit card shopping, I'd applied for seven cards and was approved for all of them. I didn't know that opening a lot of accounts in a short amount of time would lower my credit score and also make me appear to be desperate for money, which I'll talk about in a minute.

As for your credit score, each time you apply for a credit card, the issuer does a hard inquiry on your credit report. The impact isn't high, if anything at all. It's about two to five points off your credit score for each inquiry. But that's for *each* inquiry.

There's another negative side effect when you open too many accounts at once. Banks love to play amateur psychologist. While I was opening credit cards left and right simply because of the abundant opportunities, the banks were likely starting to view me as a consumer who desperately needed the credit to pay next month's rent.

When banks think you're about to fall off of your own personal fiscal cliff, they take steps to limit their exposure. And these days, the banks are highly sensitive to risk. Our spending patterns are monitored and, during the height of the Great Recession, I heard of banks closing accounts if a cardholder started shopping at discount stores. It's kind of ironic because that should also be a sign of being responsible with money.

Anyway, back then, I probably had APR (annual percentage rate) increases because of my behavior. I didn't read my mail (Mistake #8; blissful ignorance), so I had no idea what my interest rates had become.

Today, it's unlikely I'd get away with what I did in such a short amount of time. I was young with a short credit history and I opened seven accounts in rapid succession. But even if you *could* get away with it now, you never want to open so many accounts at one time.

Aside from the hit on your credit score and the impression that you're broke, you can get in a lot of trouble when you suddenly have a lot of credit. Once you're experienced with credit cards and you've proven you can use them and never carry a balance, then it's fine to have several. I know folks who have dozens of credit cards and they use spreadsheets to keep track of them. I don't recommend that, though, unless your super power is organization.

Mistake #2: Not reading the fine print

I have to confess that I never read the fine print on any of my credit cards back then. Looking back, I have to take my confession further and admit that I had no idea there even *was* fine print. I knew there were pages and pages of information that came in the mail with my new cards. I ignored it because I didn't have the patience to read it and I didn't think it could possibly be important.

I'd just tear open the big envelope and stick my hand in there like I was looking for the prize at the bottom of a Cracker Jack's box. After I got what I needed, the rest of the paper went into the circular file.

When I think back, my only defense was this: *I didn't know what I didn't know.* I had no experience with personal credit, with the exception of my Rich's card. Amazingly, I did okay with that card. It was when I graduated and had real money that the problems started.

Of course, reading the fine print isn't going to guarantee that you'll stay out of debt or that you'll pay your bill on time. But if you know you'll be paying a 19.99 percent interest rate if you don't pay off your balance every month, it might motivate you to watch your spending. The fine print tells you about fees, such as annual and foreign transaction fees. You'll also learn if the bank has a penalty rate and which circumstances will lead to you getting stuck with it. Penalty rates can be as high as a variable 29.99 percent.

If that rate doesn't scare the bejeebers out of you, then you don't understand compound interest. But don't worry, you'll learn about this in Chapter 4. And I promise it won't be painful.

Mistake #3: Buying stuff I didn't need (then buying more of it)

I started to call this one "not having a budget." Because, really, if you have a budget, there isn't usually a line item for "outrageous amounts spent on designer clothes so I feel better about myself." I worked in a corporate office with a lot of men, and I felt I needed "power" clothes and accessories to be taken seriously. These were the days of suits with huge shoulder pads.

I'm 5-foot, 2-inches tall and petite. I looked like a tiny line-backer in these suits. I'm not a psychologist, but there was clearly an emotional element to my spending. I bought one thing after another and all of it was designed to make me feel professional and credible.

At the end of the day, it doesn't matter *why* you're buying so much stuff. There's one end result when you spend more than you earn: You get into credit card debt. But there's also fallout beyond the debt itself.

One month during my spending decade, I bounced 12 checks. And to be honest, this was a total surprise to me at the time. The NSF (non-sufficient funds) fees set me back quite a bit. I actually had to stop making credit card payments for a few months (Mistake #7) so my cash flow could catch up to my monthly expenses.

If I'd had a budget, I would've known I was going into the red that month, and hopefully, stopped myself. I think budgets don't get enough attention these days. They just seem kind of dull, right? Well, that's a thing of the past. There are so many great options out there. And many of them are free.

If you don't have a budget in place, you need to sit yourself down and take a look at some of the free online money management programs. It doesn't have to be you and a spreadsheet unless that really appeals to you. Do whatever is easy for you. If it's easy to use, you'll be more likely to stick with it.

Our family uses Mint.com and we have for years. I say "our family" because we all use it. Even my youngest, my 17-year-old son, started using it when he got a part-time job. I like the user interface because it's very visual. You can set up budgets for different categories. You can look at pie charts and graphs and see where your money went that month. There are other free online money management programs out there, too. So check them out online and find one that you feel comfortable with.

One complaint I hear a lot is that having a budget is too restrictive. Nothing could be further from the truth. It actually puts you in charge. The way you spend your money reflects how you're spending your life. A budget ensures that you're spending your hard-earned money on things that matter to you.

Mistake #4: Not knowing how much I spent or where I spent it

This, of course, is related to Mistake #3. Are you starting to notice how interconnected personal finance is? A mistake in one area creates a problem in another area. It's a domino effect.

Do you know what mindful spending is? It means you pay attention to every dollar you spend. If you're on a budget and you're practicing mindful spending, you don't buy a lot of things you don't need. There's no "Oh, my God!" moment when you get your credit card statement. You already have a good idea of how much you owe before you open the envelope. Tracking your spending is the only way to know how much you spent and where you spent it. When you don't track your spending, you're on your way to debt. It's really that simple.

I just told you that I use Mint.com to budget my finances. Mint.com also lets me set up category limits and I get an e-mail when I'm approaching one of my pre-set limits. So I'm able to track my spending by category.

Here's something to keep in mind if you use your credit cards for reward points or just to postpone the expense until your statement arrives. You need a budget for each credit card. So if you declare you're going to spend $400 a month on your airline miles card to buy groceries, you need to stick to that. If you go over that amount and can't pay the balance in full when the statement arrives, you're going to pay interest expense.

So what if you *do* need to spend $50 more on groceries one week because you're having a house guest? Or maybe it's your daughter's Sweet Sixteen party? Because you have a budget, you find that extra

$50 from another category that month so you can stay on budget and still pay your bills on time.

Having a budget also gives you the go-ahead for a "budgeted splurge" item. A budgeted splurge is when you buy an item that may be a little expensive, but you've cut corners in other areas of your budget to pay for it.

Here's an example: I spent $32 last week on Givenchy mascara. I do a lot of video and TV, so I spend a lot of money on makeup. But this is part of my budget. I rarely go out to movies and I'm a pro at getting good value on groceries. I drive a nine-year-old car and I intend to drive until it literally conks out in the middle of the road.

My point is that it's okay to be a little crazy in one area, if you've made sacrifices somewhere else. The beauty of a budget is that you're making choices about how you spend your money. You spend money on things that are important to you and you don't waste it on things that aren't.

If you're about to apply for a credit card, a car loan, or a mortgage, there's another reason to have a budget for your credit cards. In Chapter 2, you'll learn how keeping a low balance on your cards helps to boost your credit scores.

Mistake #5: Carrying a balance on my credit cards

I wasn't worried the first time I couldn't pay my entire balance off. I should've been, though. I remember thinking it was not a problem and I'd pay it *all* off the next month. Yeah, that didn't happen.

This is how credit card debt starts. If my attitude had been "I can't believe I did this! I'm putting away the credit cards until I get this balance paid off," I would've nipped it in the bud right then. Instead, my attitude was "Ah, no big deal. I'll pay it off next month. In the meantime, I need a new scarf to add a little pizzazz to this outfit."

I didn't even look at how much interest I was paying. The reason was because I wasn't thinking about the effects of compound interest. I continued to buy things with my cards because I'd set that pattern for myself. Once I started carrying a balance on one card, it was a short jump to carrying a balance on another card. And then another.

Before you know it, you're carrying balances on all your credit cards and just making minimum payments. Carrying a balance becomes your "new normal" and the shock factor is gone. Don't let that happen to you.

I started my credit card blog because I wanted to help people learn how to profit from their credit cards and stay out of debt. I always have the same mantra: *Don't carry a balance on your credit card.* There are times when life gets messy and you might have to carry a balance now and then for a few months. That's fine. But have the appropriate "OMG!" reaction that I totally lacked. Step away from the credit cards and fix the money problem.

Using a credit card to get the miles or cash back is a good strategy. Or putting a large purchase on a credit card simply because you want an interest-free loan for a few weeks is fine, too. But the only way you'll profit from credit card use is if you pay your bill in full during the grace period. For those who don't know, when you use your card to make a purchase, the grace period is the amount of time you have to pay the bill before interest charges kick in.

Once you stop paying your bill in full every month, you're on a slippery slope. Imagine skiing down a snow-covered mountain at ever-increasing speed. Now imagine that without skis. Yeah, that's about how the effects of compound interest will feel.

Mistake #6: Maxing out my credit cards

You can carry a balance on your credit cards and still have a very good credit score. As long as your balances on each card are low and you pay all of your bills on time, your score won't suffer. Well, not directly related to your credit card balances, at least.

When you max out your credit cards, however, all heck breaks loose where your credit score is concerned. By maxing out, I mean spending up to (and for some, beyond) the limit on your credit card.

You have something called a "credit utilization ratio." It's the amount of credit you've used compared to the amount of credit you have available. I'll cover this in more detail in Chapter 2, but for now, all you need to know is that your credit utilization ratio should be no higher than 30 percent and preferably closer to 10 percent.

Let's look at an example. And listen, don't freak out about any of the math in this book. Trust me: My motto is that math should always be easy. No one should ever have to solve a word problem that involves determining the arrival time of trains going in opposite directions at different speeds in the rain.

Okay, here we go. Let's say you have three credit cards.

- ◆ Card A: $100 balance; $1,000 credit limit.
- ◆ Card B: $300 balance; $2,000 credit limit.
- ◆ Card C: $500 balance; $1,000 credit limit.

Your credit utilization ratio:

$900 (100 + 300 + 500) / $4,000 = .2250 = 22.5 percent

Anything under 30 percent is good, so this is acceptable. Let's say you decide to buy new furniture at a cost of $800 and put it on Card B. Card B's balance is now $1,100.

Here's your new ratio:

$1,700 ($900 + $800) / $4,000 = .425 = 42.5 percent

This is a high ratio and it has the potential to lower your FICO score. I'll get into how your FICO score is calculated in Chapter 2. Again, don't freak out. We won't be doing algebra or anything with moving trains. I'm just going to give you the basic information you need to know to stay out of trouble. And for those of you who like to dive headfirst into this stuff like me, I'll give you resources to check out.

Before we move on to Mistake #7, there's one more point to make about maxing out credit cards. Remember when I said issuers like to play amateur psychologist? If you start maxing out your cards, your bank might start thinking you're desperate for money. The banks notice when your credit score drops, too.

Unlike a real psychologist, though, they won't give you a call and ask how you're feeling today. It will more likely be a knee-jerk reaction to what they perceive is your impending financial doom. This reaction could involve increasing your interest rate. Issuers sometimes do this so they can collect as much interest as possible. You know, just in case you eventually default.

Or they might decrease your credit limit as soon as you start paying down the balance a little, which makes your utilization ratio even worse. This is a particularly depressing situation because you think you have some breathing room on that card and then— poof!—it's gone and you're maxed out again.

Mistake #7: Not paying my bills on time

As long as you're paying your bills on time, you can get away with being in debt and miserable for a long time. But once you started missing payments, there's that domino effect again.

Do you know what happens when you stop paying your credit card bill? Your account gets sold to a debt collection agency. And then you start getting calls from really mean debt collectors. When this happened to me, Caller ID wasn't widely available. If you're under 40, I'm sure you find this hard to imagine!

My only option was to let the calls go to my answering machine. I really mastered listening to a message just long enough to identify the caller. Hey, I was young and single at the time, so I was making sure I didn't miss calls from anyone I thought was dating material.

If it was a debt collector—the opposite of dating material—I'd wait for the person to leave a message and then delete it.

Do you remember when I talked about the domino effect? Well, allow me to switch metaphors for a moment because I need to create a mental image that's much stronger than dominoes.

Let's use the ocean as an example, because I just love the ocean and it's a powerful image. If there's an earthquake that is way off-shore, it creates a ripple effect that can eventually create a tsunami. Think of missing those first few payments as the earthquake. Make enough of them and, in time, you'll create a tsunami that threatens to wipe out your finances.

Here's how: A late payment can trigger the penalty rate. I've seen rates as high as 29.99 percent. If you get stuck with the penalty rate, and your payment was less than 60 days overdue, it applies to new purchases only. But if you're more than 60 days late, the penalty rate can be applied to your *entire* outstanding balance. So if you have a $2,000 balance, you're now looking at a 29.99 percent APR (assuming that's your penalty rate) on the whole dang thing.

Now, there's legislation called the Credit Card Accountability Responsibility and Disclosure Act of 2009 (Credit CARD Act) that tells issuers how they have to proceed when they penalize you for a late payment. (We'll get into that in Chapter 2.) And, of course, missed payments also shatter your credit score. It's impossible to predict how much your score will drop. But the more delinquent your payment is, the bigger the ding to your score.

Mistake #8: Ignoring debt and hoping it would magically go away

You can probably guess how well this approach went. But I'm going to share the details with you because I don't want you to ever make Mistake #8. This is the point where things get really out of control.

At the time, all seven of my credit cards were maxed out—every single one. In spite of my good salary, I couldn't keep up with the minimum payments because of a little thing called cash flow. Yeah, I didn't have any of that. After the credit card bills became overwhelming, I made a decision that was quite possibly the worst one I've ever made in my life. I stopped going to my mailbox.

For a few weeks, I was blissfully unaware of my debt. But then I crossed paths with my mailman and he ruined the imaginary life I had created. Being a friendly Southerner, I'm on a first-name basis with the entire world. I knew the guy who ran the seafood counter at the grocery store had 9-year-old twins. The couple who ran the dry cleaners were in therapy, but she was hopeful they'd stay together. The manager of my apartment building was getting a divorce. So, of course, I knew the mailman.

Because we were "friends" he had no problem telling me he'd thought I'd moved because I wasn't picking up my mail. I shamelessly told him that I'd lost my mailbox key. This is an opportune time to point out that when you're in debt, you turn into an extraordinary liar.

He suggested I walk with him to the mailbox so he could unlock it for me. He gave me all the mail currently stuffed in my box. That night, I did spend time going over my mail and trying to decide which bills to pay. I'd been threatened to have my electricity turned off, so I paid that. I paid half the minimums on my credit card bills, thinking that was better than nothing.

But would you believe that I still hadn't hit rock bottom? Amazingly, I still didn't stop using my credit cards. Instead, I made a decision to study for the CPA exam so I could get another job and make more money. Would you believe it worked? I got another job and made enough money to pay the minimums on my cards, and keep my electricity and water turned on.

Life, however, had changed drastically. I could no longer get approved for a card or get credit limit increases. And then it happened.

Everyone who's been in debt can tell you their rock-bottom moment. This is the point where they realize that their life is so screwed up they will do *anything* to fix it.

I was standing in line at Rich's to buy Ralph Lauren jeans. To my horror, my beloved Rich's department store card was declined. I never make a scene, so I left the store, went home, and called customer service. A service rep was blunt and told me my last check had bounced. And not only that, it showed up late and they'd had enough of it. Rich's had canceled my credit card account. I couldn't believe it. My favorite store.

Do you know how big a mess your credit life has to be to lose a retail credit card? A really, really big mess. This was the turning point for me. I was finally ready to take back my life. That day, I stopped using credit cards.

Mistake #9: Believing I had to keep my debt a secret

You're going to be totally shocked at what I'm about to tell you. While I was paying off my debt, I met my future husband. Well, my future second husband. I didn't tell him about my debt. When we got married in 1988, I was still paying off the debt.

Do you know when he found out? In September 2011 when I was working on my soon-to-be published essay, "Confessions of a Former Credit-Card-a-Holic." I didn't lie about it or even try to hide it. I just felt that the debt was my responsibility and mine to pay. Looking back, I was right to take responsibility and not expect anyone else to help me pay for it. But I'd never recommend this approach to anyone.

It might seem odd to list this as one of my biggest mistakes, but thinking back, it would have been so nice to have a "debt buddy" to talk to. And I'd never, ever recommend marrying someone without looking at their credit report!

We're all products of our culture, though. I was raised by parents who grew up during the Depression. They lived in a time where you pulled yourself up by your boot straps and you fixed your own problems. There was no whining.

I also grew up in the South and talking about money is a faux pas of the highest magnitude. You don't ask people how much money they make or how much their house cost. If you screw up your own finances, you sure as heck don't talk about it.

So I never, ever told anyone. My parents are gone now, but they were alive when I was going through this. I never told them because I didn't want them to worry about it. Okay, I also didn't want a lecture about responsibility.

Here's what happens when you're in debt and no one else knows. You start thinking that you're a loser and that no one else has ever gotten themselves into a mess like this. You think you're the only person alive who has ever made a mistake with money.

I've now been in the personal finance field for a long time and I know nothing could be further from the truth. A lot of people— good, decent, and smart people—end up in debt. I'm sure some of you reading this book are racking up debt right now. There's a significant part of the population who need credit cards to make ends meet every month. Listen, I'm not judging you and no one else should, either.

Whether you got into debt due to your own irresponsibility or due to unexpected events, such as being laid off, it doesn't matter. The fact is you're in this pickle, and you have to get out and reclaim your life. And you will!

Mistake #10: Not having any financial goals

I never once thought about the future when I was in my 20s. My motto was to live each day to the fullest. Actually, I carpe diem'd the hell out of each day.

Besides the power clothes and the power accessories, I also contributed to my debt by putting vacations on my credit card. I once had 10 cents in my checking account and went on a cruise to Mexico. And I can promise you that when I was in Mazatlan and dancing on a table at Senior Frog's (don't tell my kids), I wasn't the least bit concerned about my retirement fund.

If I'd had the discipline to build a rainy day fund, though, my priorities would've changed. Maybe I wouldn't have had sling-back lime stilettos in my closet that I wore exactly one time because they made me feel like I was walking on shards of glass.

And I remember the time I wanted to buy a condo. The reason I didn't buy one is because I could never get the down payment together. In retrospect, it's a good thing it didn't work out because the condo market dropped like a sack of potatoes back then. But I do think that if I'd thought more about what I wanted out of life, it would have motivated me to control my spending, save money, and invest for the future.

My spendthrift days are long gone and, these days, I take a holistic approach to credit. When you use your cards, you're not operating within a money bubble. So you need to think about where all of your money is going.

One of my favorite Yogi Berra sayings is "If you don't know where you're going, you'll end up some place else." This is really true when it comes to money. When you don't have long-term goals and a blueprint for how to get there, you don't get there. You just don't. Instead, you end up with lime-colored stilettos and credit card debt.

This won't happen to you, however, because in the next chapter you'll learn everything you need to know about your credit life. Knowledge is power. And you're about to become a very powerful consumer.

2

Your Credit Life Explained in Simple Language

D o you know what ticks me off? The way credit-related information is presented to the public. You hear all kinds of credit jargon tossed about in every article you read. Not everyone knows who the major credit bureaus are or what factors are included in your FICO score.

Sure, you can Google the terms, but who has time for that? It's difficult to master your credit life if every attempt at learning results in Googling and then Googling some more to understand the results of your last Google.

I think this is one of the reasons so many personal finance blogs popped up on the Internet in the past five years. People craved knowledge about money management, but they were tired of reading articles that made them feel like they were reading a foreign language.

This is exactly why I started my own credit card blog. After spending years and years as a finance journalist, I could see that having my own blog was the best way to share all the wacky stuff I know about credit cards. And I knew I could share it in a way that would be easy to take and even entertaining. I also noticed that a lot of credit card information on the Internet is wrong—some of it even on major financial Websites. So always be skeptical about what you're reading. And if something sounds off to you, send me an e-mail and I'll check it out.

Wouldn't it be nice to read the mail from your credit card issuer and know exactly what it means? This is the chapter that will take the mystery out of credit. This is a long chapter so I'm breaking it up into four easy-to-digest nuggets:

- The three major credit bureaus: Equifax, TransUnion, and Experian. You'll learn a no-stress way to get your free annual credit reports (the *official* ones), how to review a credit report, and the role the bureaus play when you apply for a credit card.
- How to use Websites that offer free credit scores. These aren't FICO scores, but you'll get tips on how to use these free scores to get an overview of your credit health.
- The basics of FICO scores. We'll cover the most-used score, FICO, but we'll touch on other scores, too. You'll learn where to get your FICO score, what factors go into the score, your credit utilization ratio, and more. (This is way more interesting than it sounds! No, really!)
- The highlights of the Credit CARD Act of 2009. This landmark legislation gives you consumer protections that you need to know about.

Are you ready to be the boss of your credit life? Awesome! Let's get started.

The three major credit bureaus

In the credit industry, there are three major credit bureaus: Equifax, TransUnion, and Experian. Some consumers think that the credit bureaus are involved in the decision-making process when you apply for a credit card. But they aren't at all.

The bureaus simply collect credit information about you. Your lenders report your payment history to one or more of the credit bureaus. So, for example, if you have three credit cards, your payment history is reported to the bureaus as a revolving account. If you have a car loan, your lender reports that as an installment loan account.

The bureaus keep track of your payment history, as well as how many accounts you have, what type of accounts you have (revolving, installment, etc.), the length of time you've had credit, and if there are any late payments or judgments against you. When you apply for a credit card, the bureaus are the middle men in the operation.

What happens when you apply for a credit card

When you apply for credit, the lender will "pull" one of your credit reports to look at your credit history. You usually won't know which credit bureau they'll use. For years, folks have tried to pin down which credit bureau is used by each major bank. But the truth is that they know we all do this. They switch it up now and then, so you never really know.

All this means is that they request your credit history (and a credit score) from a credit bureau. Now, this pull can either be a "soft inquiry" or a "hard inquiry." A soft inquiry is when a lender is confirming your identity or trying to pre-qualify you for a credit card.

This isn't a line-by-line read of your report. Soft pulls don't hurt your credit score at all. When you request your own credit report, this has the effect of a soft pull. So you don't have to worry about hurting your score when you request your own report.

On the other hand, a hard inquiry means the lender is looking at your report in an effort to determine if you qualify for a credit card or a loan you've applied for. Hard inquiries *do* impact your credit score. Each hard inquiry can reduce your score by two to five points. Usually, one hard inquiry isn't cause for concern. If you apply for a lot of credit cards at one time, however, it can create a significant drop in your score.

So, to make a decision, a lender reviews your credit report, your credit score, and the information you provided on your application. If you're approved for the credit card, you'll get a letter letting you know. The last time I applied for a card, I got an approval via e-mail. Then, a few days later, I received a letter that included the disclosure statements, my credit limit, and details about the rewards program.

My last application for a credit card had a happy ending. But as you know, I had my share of denials during my spendthrift days. In 2011, new rules were put in place about what consumers had a right to know if they were denied credit.

Your rights if your credit card application is denied

What happens if you're not approved? Well, first you will probably feel awful. It's hard not to take these things personally. I know I took it personally, even though I deserved to be denied a credit card at the time! But the best thing to do is to shake off the unpleasant feeling and read the "adverse action notice" that you got in the mail. The Fair Credit Reporting Act (FCRA) requires creditors and lenders to send the adverse action notice to explain why you were denied credit. It can be in the form of a letter or delivered by phone.

In the adverse action notice, the lender must tell you the reason you were denied and which credit bureau provided the credit report that was used to make the decision. You'll also receive the contact information for the bureau.

Now, this is very important: You're told that you can get a free credit report from the bureau that provided your credit report to the lender. You have to get this report within 60 days and I urge you to do so. Why? Well, there could be inaccurate information on the report that contributed to your denial. This happens more often than you know. A recent Federal Trade Commission study found that one out of every five consumers had errors on one of their three credit reports. And get this: 5 percent had errors that were significant enough to result in less favorable terms for credit.

If you do discover that your report has an error or is incomplete in some way, you have a right to dispute the decision. So be proactive and check your report, because you never know what you might find. If the denial had nothing to do with information in your credit report, you'll be given the reason. But in this situation, you won't have access to a free report from the bureau in question.

Anyway, you will also get a few details about the credit score that was used to make the decision. Here's the information you'll get about the score:

- The name of the bureau that provided the credit file that was used to calculate the score.

- The most recent credit score (and the date it was created) that was given to the lender from the credit reporting agency. The lender requests the score for the purpose of evaluating the consumer for credit.

- You won't get the name of the scoring model used, but you'll receive a range of credit scores that the model uses. Hint: You can figure out the model by the range. (More on that later.)

- Up to four key factors that may have negatively affected your credit score. An interesting note about the key factors is that they must be listed in order of importance based on their effect on your credit score.

Now if you get turned down for a credit card, you'll do two things. First, take a deep breath and stay calm. Second, read the adverse action letter so you know what steps to take to fix your credit problem.

How to get your free credit reports (the "official" ones)

Have you seen those commercials about getting your free credit report? All you have to do is go to FreeCreditReport.com where they say you can get your free credit report (instantly!) if you fork over one dollar. And you get your free credit score, too. Well, forget all that.

You automatically get signed up for a credit monitoring service (but you do get a 7-day free trial). The report you get is from Experian. The score you get is the Experian Plus Score Model. It states that this score is for educational purposes and *not the score used by lenders* (italics are mine). I do commend Experian for being upfront that this isn't your FICO score. This is what we call a FAKO score. (Cute, huh?) I'll explain FICO and FAKO scores in a minute. For now, let's finish talking about your credit report.

Here's the absolutely official Website for getting your official free credit report: *www.annualcreditreport.com*. This is the only service that's authorized by all three major credit bureaus—Equifax, TransUnion, and Experian—for this purpose. You are entitled to one free credit report from each of the major bureaus every 12 months. You can make the request through this Website and, really, it couldn't be easier.

You can order online (it's a secure site) or you can request your report via phone or have it mailed. Note that requests by phone or mail can take 15 days to be processed after your request.

What to look for in your credit report

Because each lender makes its own decision regarding how many credit bureaus it reports to, your credit reports will vary from bureau to bureau. One lender might report your car loan payment history to Equifax and Experian, but not to TransUnion. Another lender might report your history only to TransUnion. Yet another might report your credit card payment history to all three bureaus.

The report from each credit bureau also looks different. But there is some basic information that's common to all three. They will all have a *report number*. This number is located near your personal information. If you have an issue with your report, you'll need this number when you contact the bureau.

So let's take a quick look at a few major areas and I'll give you some tips about what to look for. Note that the order of these sections will vary a little by bureau. Do a line-by-line review and verify that the information in these sections is accurate.

- **Personal information.** This section contains details such as your name, your social security number, your date of birth, your current address, and your previous addresses. You'll also see your employment data, both current and previous.

- **Negative accounts or items.** If you have any collection accounts, late payments, or any past due accounts, you'll see them here.

- **Public records.** Here, you'll find bankruptcies, judgments, or liens.

- **Open accounts, credit items, or accounts in good standing.** Your credit accounts, including your credit cards, mortgage, car loans, and personal loans are listed here. Other information includes your credit limits and recent balances. Note that there are often timing issues and your balance on your credit report might not reflect the most up-to-date information.

- **Credit history requests.** You'll see which creditors requested your credit report. The purpose of the request is also listed. For example, if you're trying to rent an apartment, your potential landlord might check your credit report to review your payment history.

Remember: The information and the way it's presented will vary, so take a flexible approach with each report.

What if you find an error?

If you find an error, contact the creditor in question to let them know and send a certified letter with a return receipt requested to the credit bureau that has the error on your report. The credit reporting agency must investigate the dispute within 30 days (unless it decides the dispute is frivolous). In your letter, include copies of any relevant documents that support your case.

It's stressful to figure out how to word something like this, isn't it? That's why I've included a sample letter on the opposite page. When the bureau investigates the item, they have to forward the documentation you provided to show the information is inaccurate.

The creditor in question has to investigate and then report back to the credit reporting company. If the creditor does determine that the information is inaccurate, then the creditor has to notify all three credit bureaus so they can fix the information that's on your credit report.

At that point, the credit bureau must give you the results of the investigation in writing and give you a free copy of the corrected report. And just so you know, this doesn't count as one of your free reports.

The Federal Trade Commission (FTC) has a wonderful consumer education section. Check out their Website, (*www.consumer.ftc.gov/*), to get more information about disputing errors on credit reports.

Credit Report Errors: Sample Dispute Letter

Date
Your name
Your address, City, State, Zip Code

Dear Sir or Madam:

I am sending this certified letter to inform you that there is (are) an error(s) on my credit report(s). I have enclosed documentation (for example, a copy of the credit report) that contains the information I am disputing. The disputed item(s) are circled.

The information states that (identify the incorrect information by using the creditor's name and the details of the error that's on your report; for example, a report of a late payment that you know didn't happen). This item is incorrect (or incomplete) because (explain why it's inaccurate or incomplete). I am making a formal request that the item(s) be removed (or revised to make it accurate, whichever the case may be).

I have also enclosed documentation (for example, payment records and court documents) that supports my position that the information in my credit file is inaccurate.

Please investigate this (these) matter(s) and (delete or correct) the inaccurate information. I would appreciate it if you would do this as soon as possible.

Thank you for your time and prompt attention to this matter.

Sincerely,
Your name

Enclosures: list the number and name of each report or document that you've included.

Signs of identity theft

If you see an account that you didn't open or charges on a credit card that you didn't make, these could be signs of identity theft. You'll want to go immediately to the FTC's Website and follow the steps for reporting identity theft. But here's a summary of what you should expect to do if this happens to you.

First, ask one of the three credit bureaus to place a fraud alert on your file. That bureau is required to tell the other two. Fraud alerts are free, by the way. This step alone makes it difficult for the thief to do further damage. You will have to renew the alert in 90 days, but your goal right now is damage control. You should also call the business involved and talk to someone in its fraud department.

Next, you need to order all three credit reports. And thankfully, when you place a fraud alert on your file, you're entitled to free reports.

Being an identity theft victim is a pain in the neck. Plus, it can cause a lot of damage. I once got a call from a bank customer service rep asking me about a late payment. Fortunately, this was decades after my credit card disaster years, so I actually knew which accounts I had opened and that they were all in good standing.

I told the caller that I didn't open an account at his bank. Then I asked him to give me his phone number and name so I could call back and ask for him. I wanted to make sure he was an employee of the bank and not a scammer. It all checked out and I realized my identity had been stolen. It was a creepy feeling. I felt violated, like someone had been in my house and gone through my things. This was before I was checking my credit report regularly. If I had been, I would have spotted it.

As I already mentioned, the FTC Website tells you exactly what to do and how to do it. I also like IdentityTheft911.com as a resource because it has an excellent Knowledge Center on the Website.

One thing you can do to protect yourself is to guard your CVV (card verification value) number. This is the number that's important during card-not-present transactions, such as ordering pizza over the phone or online. The system will verify that your card matches the number you gave so they know you're the one holding your card, not a thief. The CVV on MasterCard, Visa, and Discover are located on the back of the card, as shown here. The CVV for American Express is four digits and it's located on the front of the card.

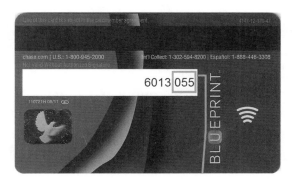

Consumer Financial Protection Bureau

If you try to dispute the error and you aren't getting any satisfaction, then contact the Consumer Financial Protection Bureau (CFPB). Filing a complaint is a painless process. But remember that this is a government agency so don't expect your problem to get resolved overnight.

When you file a complaint, you'll receive e-mail updates and you can even log in to the system to track your complaint. The CFPB forwards your complaint to the business involved. Hopefully, getting a consumer watchdog involved can resolve the situation. Sometimes a business just needs a little more incentive to do the right thing.

What about your free FICO score?

It doesn't exist. If you're on a Website and your credit score appears to be free, then it's not a FICO score. In many cases, you have to read the fine print carefully to avoid signing up for a credit monitoring service. Now, there are Websites that offer free scores and you don't have to sign up for anything. It is truly free.

However, these aren't FICO scores. They're the FAKO scores I alluded to earlier. But even though they aren't FICO scores, you can still get some value from them. Most of these Websites offer an analysis of the score you receive, and that's where you get your value.

You have dozens of credit scores

Most people are very surprised to find out that there isn't one credit score. There are several different credit score "models" that are used. There are credit score models that are designed to assess risk for different types of credit. For example, FICO introduced its new Mortgage Credit Score in 2012. This score is designed, obviously, for mortgage lenders. There's even an auto insurance score that's designed to predict the likelihood that you'll file an insurance claim.

A lender might choose the score that's most applicable to what you're applying for. Although the factors credit scores use aren't that different, they might weigh each item differently. This can create a lot of different scores. About 90 percent of lenders use the FICO score, but as you've just seen, there are also varieties of FICO scores. I'm going into the most detail about FICO scores because that's the score you need to be most concerned about.

First, though, let's take a look at a few of the most common scores—often called "educational scores"—that are out there. I want to make sure you understand the difference between FICO scores and the rest of the pack. So you understand the difference in the number ranges, FICO scores range from 300–850.

VantageScore. The latest version is VantageScore 3.0. This score ranges from 300–850. Earlier VantageScore models had a range of 500–900. VantageScore was created in collaboration among all three major credit bureaus. On the surface, it appears to make the scores easy to compare.

However, I worry that it would create a different type of confusion. VantageScore weighs certain factors differently than FICO, so you shouldn't expect the scores to be close to the same. VantageScore focuses more on the past two years of your credit history.

VantageScore is also said to be easier on those who have thin files (not a lot of credit). The FICO score only uses the past six months in its calculations. So if you're new to credit, you might not even generate a credit score. The VantageScore 3.0 model considers at least 24 months of credit history, which means about 27 to 30 million more consumers actually get a credit score. If you'd like more details, check out *www.vantagescore.com*. And the new 3.0 version is said to take a kinder view on debts that go into collection as long as the current balance is zero.

The problem for those who benefit from a high VantageScore is that if your issuer uses a FICO score, which is likely, you could overestimate your credit status. So don't rely on your VantageScore as the only true indicator of your overall credit health.

Experian Plus Score. This score is a proprietary model created by Experian. The range for this score is 330 to 830.

Equifax Beacon Score. This is a proprietary model created by Equifax. The range for this score is 300 to 850.

TransUnion TransRisk Score. This is a proprietary model created by TransUnion. The range for this score is 300 to 850.

FreeCreditScore.com. I wanted to bring this up and explain it because I get so many questions about free scores, especially regarding this Website. This Website, and FreeCreditReport.com, is owned by Experian. The score you get is the Experian Plus Score Model. When you order your "free" credit score, you're signing up for a seven-day trial membership, which includes fraud alerts, ID protection, and such. The cost is $17.99 per month, and you have to cancel during the trial period to avoid being charged.

Where you can get free educational scores

Now you understand that there are credit scores that are for educational purposes only. This is very important to know so that you don't misinterpret your true credit standing.

I spent two hours one afternoon signing up for accounts on these three Websites: Credit Karma, Credit.com, and Credit Sesame. I received credit scores and I also got some excellent information about the factors that go into my credit score. But the scores I got were *vastly* different from each other. Of course they're different; they come from different bureaus and they use different scoring models. But here's how you use these Websites:

- Take a look at the "grades" you get for each of the factors that go into your score. This is where the value lies.
- Along the same lines, these reports give you an idea of your credit health.
- Don't use the score you get to determine if you can qualify for a specific credit card. We'll use a FICO score for that.
- Don't buy credit monitoring. You'll see a hard sell on all these Websites.
- Don't buy a credit report on these Websites.

Here's a brief overview of each Website, including which scoring model and credit bureau they use to get your information. Note that the score and credit bureau used is subject to change.

Credit Karma. This Website offers a free "Credit Report Card" and you get letter grades on a variety of factors, such as credit card utilization, percent of payments made on time, credit inquiries, and so on.

Score used: TransRisk Score from TransUnion. The score is based on your TransUnion credit report.

You can now connect to your accounts using the new Credit Karma Insight if you'd like to view your finances in one place. I didn't connect my accounts because I use Mint.com for my money management.

Credit.com. This Website also has a free tool called "Credit Report Card" that initially offered an Experian score, but has switched to VantageScore 3.0.

Score used: VantageScore 3.0, using the Experian credit file.

It literally took seconds to sign up. I was asked a few identifying questions and then I was done.

You receive a letter grade on these categories: payment history, debt usage, credit age, account mix, and inquiries. You can look at each category in greater detail if you choose. The user interface is excellent. The layout is pleasant, and it's easy to understand the explanations of each factor that goes into your score.

Credit Sesame. This Website offers a free "Credit Score," but you get much more than that. You also get an analysis of your credit and debt.

Score used: Experian Plus Credit Score, which, of course, uses your Experian credit file.

You can also add financial goals, which is a nice feature. There's also an abundance of graphs and charts and that makes it easy to understand the numbers. As well, Credit Sesame has an excellent Mortgage Loan Research Center if you're looking for a mortgage or to refinance your current mortgage.

Do-it-yourself credit monitoring

Seriously, most people do not need a credit monitoring service. There are exceptions, of course. Do you have a soon-to-be ex on a vendetta? If you have a joint account that hasn't been closed yet, then this is a situation that might benefit from a monitoring service. Also, if you've had a recent experience with identity theft, this is another situation where you need to be extra vigilant.

But many people get talked into these services, or accidentally sign up for them when they get free scores on Websites. It's often a waste of money. You can monitor your own credit by checking your online accounts daily. Is that too much? Okay, I'll let you slide to twice a week.

Do you remember the free annual credit reports that really are free on AnnualCreditReport.com? Spread them out. Get one every four months and this kind of "monitors" your credit over the course of the year. Between that and checking your credit card accounts frequently, you should be in good shape in regard to detecting fraud.

What you need to know about FICO scores

Credit card issuers use FICO scores more frequently than any other score. For our purposes, I'm going to focus on the "generic" FICO score. As I already said, there are several versions of FICO scores. But there are basic factors that are considered across the scores.

If you'd like to really dig into the details, go to MyFICO.com. This is a great resource for educating yourself about credit scores and about credit in general. You can buy your FICO score on MyFICO.com. Ignore the offer for the "free" score. You get signed up for a monitoring service and then you'd have to remember to cancel it before the trial period ends.

What you want is the FICO Standard score and it's $19.99. You can get your FICO standard score pulling information from Equifax, TransUnion, or Experian. FICO scores based on Experian data have not been available to consumers for several years. Just recently, Experian and FICO started offering the score again. That's the way it should be, because consumers should have access to FICO scores from all three bureaus.

If you make a mistake in a particular area, it's impossible to know the exact impact on your score. The answer for one person's profile will not be accurate for everyone else's profile. So rather than try to guess what you can get away with, focus on each of these areas. If you excel in each area, you will most likely have a good score.

Basically, these are guidelines to pay attention to. The weight of each factor could also vary by each profile. Here are the major factors that make up your FICO score.

Payment history: 35 percent. The score considers your payment history on all of your credit cards, installment loans, mortgages, personal loans, and so on. The obvious thing to do here is to make sure you pay your bills on time. And as you can see, it's not just about paying your credit card bills on time. You need to pay *all* of your bills on time.

Do you know what else matters? The details on how late a payment is. The score considers how late they were, how many times it's happened, how recently it happened, and even the amount owed. Some things (like a bankruptcy or a judgment) are serious and really do impact your score. But take solace in knowing that the impact of such things lessens as time passes.

Amounts owed: 30 percent. Here's where credit utilization comes in. This is the amount of credit used compared to the amount of credit available on your credit cards. The standard advice is to keep the ratio under 30 percent. But to get the most benefit from this part of your score, keep it under 10 percent.

The other things that the score looks at within this category are the amount owed on different types of accounts (such as credit cards and installment loans), the number of accounts with balances (a large number of accounts with balances indicates high risk), and how much is left on any installment loan (like a car loan).

Length of credit history: 15 percent. A longer credit history is good for your score. Here's what is considered: how long you've had accounts, the age of the oldest account, age of the newest account, and the average of all your accounts.

Types of credit used: 10 percent. The score likes it when you have a good mix. For example, if you have credit card accounts (this is revolving credit), installment loans, mortgage loans, and personal loans. You don't have to have all these accounts, just a good mix, such as credit cards and installment loans.

I financed a used car for a short time a few years ago because I wanted an installment loan in my profile. I hadn't had a car loan in 25 years. My score took a hit at first because of the debt, but paying it down quickly ended up boosting my score. Note, however, that people with no credit cards are considered higher risk. Is that fair? Of course not! That's just how it's perceived.

New credit: 10 percent. The score frowns upon too many new accounts, especially in a short amount of time. This tends to have a greater impact on consumers who don't have a long credit history. Now, the score does know if you're rate shopping for a mortgage and it lets that slide.

If you open several credit cards in a short time, though, it doesn't let that slide. Your score gets dinged for every inquiry. And although inquiries stay on your credit report for two years, the calculation for the FICO score only considers inquiries from the last 12 months.

How do you generate a FICO score?

You get a social security number when you're born in the United States, but you don't get a FICO score. In fact, you have to actually start from scratch and earn your score. So when someone says their FICO score is zero, they're sadly misinformed. They have none at all because the lowest FICO score is 300. Your credit report must have these minimum requirements to generate a score:

- ◆ An account that's been open for a minimum of six months.
- ◆ An undisputed account that has been reported to a credit bureau within the past six months.
- ◆ No indication that you're dead. Seriously, your credit report should be void of any signs that you're deceased.

How a FICO Score Breaks Down

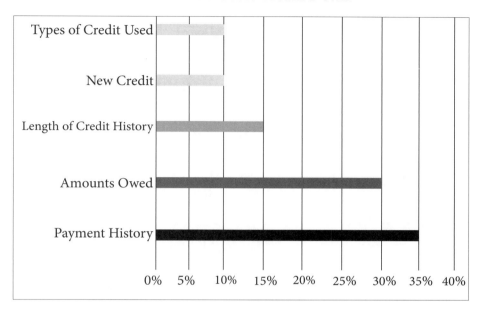

Regarding the last point, MyFICO.com notes that if you share an account with another person, this may affect you if the other account holder is reported as dead. The message is clear: Don't depend on dead people for a good FICO score.

Things that (surprisingly) don't affect your FICO score

Now you can relax and rejoice in all the things you don't have to worry about. I think you'll be surprised at some of the things that are *not* included in the calculation of your FICO score. The FICO score really tries hard to avoid discrimination. I also have a feeling some of these points might trigger a "Thank you, God!" response, too. You'll see what I mean.

- **Your race, religion, marital status, sex, age, and life philosophy.** The FICO score doesn't care who you are or what you think. In fact, it doesn't care if you think at all. FICO doesn't care if you post drunken photos of yourself on Facebook. But your current employer might.

- **Your income level.** Some people assume that if you make a lot of money, you get a higher FICO score. The truth is that it doesn't matter if you make $10,000 a year or $1,000,000 a year. The FICO score doesn't care if you're a neurosurgeon or a waiter. And this is exactly the way it should be.

- **Your bank account totals.** The score doesn't care if you even *have* a bank account, let alone how much money you have in your checking account. The FICO score also doesn't judge you if you don't have a savings account.

- **You pay interest on your credit card balances.** Remember the utilization ratio? It's the amount of credit used compared to the amount of credit you have available. As long as your ratio is low, the FICO score doesn't care if you pay interest on your balances. But as your credit card expert and friend, I'd like you to stop that.

- **You don't have a job.** The FICO score doesn't consider your work status. You don't get credit for a high-paying job and you don't get penalized for having no job at all.

- **You're receiving public assistance.** The score doesn't care if you're unemployed and if you receive unemployment benefits or food stamps.

- **You've been to a credit counselor.** Don't worry about this. The score doesn't care if you get counseling. This is how it should be. No one should be penalized for trying to fix their credit.

There are others, too, but I think you get my drift. Whenever you're wondering what's included, look at the handy dandy FICO chart I've provided on the previous page for you as a reminder.

What is the score range for excellent credit?

Like everything related to credit scores, this is a bit of a gray area. Every expert you ask might say something different. And when the economy shifts, the cutoff for excellent credit can also change. So, keeping all of this in mind, you can see the value for credit ranges in the following chart.

What's a Good FICO Score?

Excellent Credit	750+*
Good Credit	700–749
Fair Credit	650-699
Poor Credit	600-649
Bad Credit	Below 599

When the economy is going well, 720+ might be enough for the best rates.

Furthermore, when the economy is in good shape and credit loosens up, a 720 score is often good enough for the best credit card offers, depending upon your specific credit profile. And fair credit is often referred to as average credit.

Don't obsess over your score

It might seem strange for me to spend so much ink on this and then say: *Don't sweat it!* I want you to understand credit scores, especially FICO scores, so you can make smart decisions with your credit. But I don't want you to check your free scores every day or pay for a FICO score every month just to see where you stand.

And here's the thing to remember: The scores fluctuate all the time. When you pay for your FICO score, you're getting a snapshot of what your score is that day and at that time. Even the next day, your score could be different if a credit bureau has reported new information.

Now, if you're planning to refinance your mortgage or open a new credit card account, then that's a good time to check. But from a day-to-day standpoint, your credit score doesn't need to be on the top of your mind. Be informed and check it before you do something significant. But don't obsess. Seriously, folks, it's like trying to catch the wind.

Another free and easy way to estimate your credit score

You know all those pre-screened credit card offers you get in the mail? Take a look at the offers. If you're getting offers to apply for credit cards that require excellent credit, then your score is probably in the excellent category or close to it.

If you're getting offers for cards that require only average credit, then that's what you are. Not you personally, but your score. This isn't a foolproof method, but it gives you a hint about your standing.

And while we're talking about pre-screened offers, now is a good time to explain what that really means. Banks get mailing lists from a variety of sources, including the credit bureaus. So they can get lists of consumers who have excellent credit, good credit, fair credit, and so on.

These lists help banks target their mailings to the correct demographic. But these offers don't mean you'll be approved for sure—even if it says "you're pre-approved." All this means is that you appear to fit their target market and you're invited to apply for their card. It's a little misleading, don't you think?

Credit CARD Act of 2009

Now, don't skip this section! I know you were going to. Legislation doesn't sound too sexy, does it? Stick with me for a few more minutes because you received some important protections with the Credit CARD Act. You need to know what these are, so you know your rights. Then if your rights get trampled on, you can take care of business.

Plus, you can show off your knowledge at cocktail parties. You might think I'm being sarcastic, but I'm not. When folks find out I'm a credit card diva, they want to pick my brain for what feels like hours. This has happened to me at parties, while getting a pedicure, in line at the grocery store, and at my son's baseball games. I'm pretty friendly and I talk to everyone, so it's partly my fault that I get drawn into these advice sessions.

I guess it's because almost all of us have credit cards and almost all of us find it a frustrating experience at times. But I don't mind because it feels great to help people understand this stuff. Heck, that's why I have a blog about credit cards.

Just a few highlights

The actual legislation that's entitled "Credit Card Accountability Responsibility and Disclosure Act of 2009" is 33 pages of the smallest print you've ever seen. Several Websites have condensed the material into digestible pieces.

The Federal Reserve has a pretty good WYNTK (What You Need to Know) page, although I did call them once to tell them there were two things they needed to clarify. Would you believe they ignored me? It's okay. I got over it in about a nanosecond. I'll explain it in the highlights section.

Keep in mind that these protections are only available if you are using consumer credit cards. Business credit cards are not covered. I'll talk about that more in Chapter 8. Here are the highlights:

No APR increases during the first 12 months. This was an important rule because there were instances of "bait and switch." You got offered one low APR (annual percentage rate) and thought that was the go-to rate, and then *wham!* It went up 10 percentage points two months later. Exceptions:

- Your APR is variable and the prime rate goes up.
- Introductory rates have to be in place for six months before you have to pay the go-to rate.
- You're in a workout agreement and you don't pay as agreed.
- You're more than 60 days late with a payment.

Increasing APRs or fees. Your credit card company has to give you a 45-day advance notice if it plans to do the following:

- ◆ Increase your interest rate.
- ◆ Change or add fees (for example, add an annual fee).
- ◆ Make major changes to the terms and conditions.

The reason you get a notice is so you have the option to cancel your card rather than accept the changes. But there are consequences to closing accounts, and we'll be talking about that later on.

As well, if you have a balance and you decide to close your account, the card issuer can require you to pay the balance off in five years or double the percentage used to calculate your minimum monthly payment. All I'm saying is, don't have a knee-jerk reaction because they just ticked you off. Look at your options and think it over.

Exceptions to the 45-day rule. The card issuer does *not* have to send you a 45-day notice to let you know about APR increases or fee changes if any of the following are true:

- ◆ Your introductory rate expires.
- ◆ You have a variable APR and the prime rate goes up.
- ◆ You're in a workout agreement and you haven't paid as agreed.

Big freakin' loophole. This is the issue I called teh Fed about. You do, indeed, get 45 days notice of an increase in your APR. But that only means that you get 45 days before you have to actually *pay* the extra money. Interest on new purchases *starts accruing* 14 days after the postmark date on the envelope of the notice that was sent to you.

Another big freakin' loophole. If you're more than 60 days late with a payment, your new APR can be applied to your entire outstanding balance. The 45 days notice? You get it, but it only means that you get 45 days before you have to actually pay at the higher rate. Interest on your entire balance starts accruing 14 days after the postmark date on the envelope of the notice that was sent to you.

Reviewing an APR increase. Before the CARD Act, your credit card issuer wasn't required to reconsider your rate increase. Now, the issuer is required to review your account every six months to determine if your old APR should be reinstated. This is an area that a lot of consumers as well as the media misunderstand. The issuer is not *required* to reinstate your old rate. It is only required to *review* your account.

This is a situation where I recommend you take a ninja approach. If you've gotten a penalty rate, contact your issuer after six months to make sure it is going to review your account. If the reasons for receiving the increase are still there, don't expect your rate to go back to normal. But if you've really improved your credit history, fight for the right to have your old APR back.

Payment allocation. If you pay more than the minimum payment on your credit card bill, the excess amount is applied to the balance with the highest APR. There is an exception if you made a purchase using a deferred interest plan. So speak to your card issuer first if you plan to pay more than the minimum on your other credit cards.

Over-the-limit transactions. The Act put the kibosh on over-the-limit fees. If you want the merchant to accept your card even if you're over your credit limit, then you have to tell your card issuer. Otherwise, if a transaction would take you over your limit, your card could be declined.

If you opt in to allowing transactions that take you over your credit limit, your credit card issuer can charge you a fee. Take my advice here. Don't opt in to go over your limit. If you're that maxed out, you need to take a step back from credit cards.

Protections for underage consumers. If you are under 21, you have to be able to show that you have the income to pay back any debts you incur. Otherwise, you'll need a cosigner to get approved for a credit card account.

Caps on high-fee cards. Credit card issuers can't charge you fees that exceed more than 25 percent of your initial credit limit. For example, if your initial credit limit is $1,000, the fees for the first year can't exceed $250.

First Premier used to charge a $95 processing fee plus a $75 annual fee. With a credit limit of only $300, this exceeded the new rule. First Premier legally challenged this rule by saying that "up-front fees," such as the processing fee, shouldn't be included in this rule. Unfortunately, First Premier prevailed, so folks with bad credit who need a credit card have to be careful when dealing with these types of issuers.

No universal default. Before the CARD Act, universal default was not prohibited. This was the practice of increasing a cardholder's rate if the individual made late payments to other creditors such as a mortgage lender. It's hard to believe this was allowed for so long.

No inactivity fees. You can't be charged a fee for not using your card. Some card agreements, though, state that you can lose your rewards if your card is inactive for a specified period of time.

To check out the Federal Reserve's handy guide to the CARD Act, go to: *www.federalreserve.gov/consumerinfo/wyntk_creditcardrules.htm.*

3

What's Your Credit Card Personality?

'll bet I know what you're thinking. You're thinking this is probably another weird quiz that tells you about your personality based on your choice of potato chips.

Seriously, that stuff gets old, doesn't it? This quiz is different. It's the opposite of the chip-type quiz. You know your personality and habits better than anyone else on the planet. So this quiz uses what you know about your personal style and money habits as the basis for picking the right type of card for you. Here's the tough part: You have to tell the unvarnished truth. No one else has to know your answers. This is between you and the book.

One of the reasons why research is sometimes worthless is because people answer questions in a way that makes them look good. So if you feel tempted to answer the way you think you *should* answer as opposed to being brutally honest, then write your choices on a piece of paper. That way, they're not written in the book and you don't have to worry about anyone else seeing your answers. I tend to do this anyway because I treat my books like they're priceless treasures. My family has so many books I turned my living room into a home library. I just love books.

Note to readers who have never had a credit card: I'm so glad you're reading this book! I have a whole chapter just for you. Feel free to take the test, though, to gauge what your personality might become after you gain experience with credit. And be sure you read the section that describes each card type before you go on to Chapter 4.

Credit card personality quiz

1. When your credit card statement arrives, you:

a. Immediately feel nauseous after looking at it. You then hide it from your significant other while you work on your cover story.

b. Open it right away to review the charges and confirm that the balance is what you think it should be. If everything looks okay, you plan to pay the balance in full.

c. Look at the minimum payment amount and plan to pay it online before the due date.

d. Put it in the "incoming mail" area in the kitchen that includes sales flyers from nine months ago. You'll look at it later. *Much* later.

e. Look at your balance and pay more than the minimum. You plan to cut back on spending and pay the rest of the balance off next month.

2. You get two credit card offers in the mail. One is for a rewards card and one is a low-interest card with no rewards. The first thing you do is:

a. Immediately hop online and apply for both cards. The mall awaits!

b. Decide to apply for the low-APR card. Your rewards cards both have high APRs and you think it's a good idea to have a low APR card just for emergencies.

c. You're already carrying a balance on three cards. You don't want to be tempted with more credit so you put the envelopes in the "to be shredded" pile.

d. Look at the rewards card APR and it's a little high. You decide to pass.

e. Get excited about the cards, but then realize you have your neighbor's mail. Now you know the neighbor has good credit.

3. If someone asked you if you know what your APR is and what your balances are on all of your credit cards, you'd say:

a. Of course I do! Doesn't everyone?

b. What's an APR?

c. I know my credit balances because my credit limits are pretty low.

d. Yes, I know my APRs because if I have to carry a balance, I use the card with the lowest rate.

e. Yes, I know the APRs because it's stressing me out. I also know the balances because they match my credit limit.

4. Your thoughts about the role of credit cards in your life are:

a. I have credit cards so I can travel for free.

b. Credit cards are great! I can buy things I want even if I don't have the cash. I can pay the bill off over the next year (or three).

c. If it weren't for credit cards, I couldn't pay my medical bills right now.

d. I'm using credit cards a little bit every month so I can improve my credit score.

e. Credit cards help me manage my cash flow. There are some months that I have to carry a balance, but I try to pay it all off the next month.

5. How long has it been since you checked your credit report?

a. I check it when I think about it—usually once a year.

b. I check all three credit reports every year. I check for fraud and make sure there are no errors that could drag down my credit scores.

c. It's been way over a year. I've missed a few payments and I'm afraid to see the current status. I'll check it as soon as my finances get better and I can pay the bills.

d. I checked it three months ago because I'm worried about my credit scores.

e. What's a credit report?

6. Do you know your credit score?

a. I check free credit scores online to see if my score has gone up enough to get an unsecured credit card. I do this a lot, hoping it will get better.

b. Isn't that the same thing as a credit report? You just asked me that question!

c. I pay for a credit score once a year when I get one of my credit reports. I have excellent credit!

d. I'm afraid to see what my current score is. It used to be excellent, but not anymore.

e. I know that my credit is in the "good range."

7. Your TV is getting old and you want to upgrade to a really nice big-screen HDTV. There's a sale at Best Buy. Your first step is:

a. You'd love to buy this, and if you had a card with a zero percent APR on purchases, you'd so do it. You'll have the money for the TV in three months, but because you can't pay it off quickly, you don't buy the TV.

b. You'd love a newer and bigger HDTV, but because you're thinking of selling the one you have to pay your bills, it doesn't really make sense. You hope your neighbors buy it, though, so you can watch the big game at their house.

c. You go buy it. You're not sure when you can pay off the debt, but you deserve a new TV, and in the global scheme of things, that's all that really matters.

d. You don't have the cash and you don't have a credit card with a limit that's high enough to cover the purchase. You briefly consider getting it financed at Best Buy, but you decide that this isn't a smart move.

e. You decided to use your latest credit card, which has a zero percent introductory interest rate on purchases. You put the TV on your card, and simultaneously also meet the spending requirement to get a $200 sign-up bonus. You love it when this happens!

8. Your family wants to take a beach vacation, but you don't have the cash to pay for everything in full. You get your work bonus before the bill will be due, though, and paying off the balance won't be a problem. You:

a. Get a cash advance on your credit card. You'll pay the bill whenever.

b. Use your rewards card to get the miles because you know your bonus will show up before the credit card bill is due. If the bonus is late, you'll be okay because you have a rainy day fund to bridge the time gap.

c. Are so tempted to go because you need a vacation. But your balances right now are higher than normal, so you reluctantly—and with a heavy sigh—pass on the beach.

d. Wish you were heading to the beach. But you need to use your bonus to pay down your debt. Maybe you'll go next year when life calms down.

e. Decide to start saving money to take a trip next year. You're trying to keep your credit balances low to boost your credit score. Besides, you don't have a rainy day fund and it seems risky.

9. Your credit card issuer raises your interest rate. You:

a. Call your issuer and beg them to lower your rate. Your credit score is plummeting and you need this card. You're referred to the hardship department and they work out a payment plan with you.

b. Decide that it doesn't matter because you aren't carrying a balance anyway. You're biding your time until your score is high enough for an unsecured credit card.

c. Call the issuer and inform them that you're holding credit card offers from two other issuers who would love to have you as a cardholder. You get off the phone with a rate that has a lower APR than your original rate.

d. Decide to stop using that credit card if you think you'll carry a balance. Instead, you'll use a card with a lower rate.

e. Have no idea that your interest rate has been increased.

Scoring: Add up the points based on your answers. 1. a=3, b=1, c=4, d=5, e=2; 2. a=5, b=1, c=4, d=2, e=3; 3. a=1, b=5, c=3, d=2, e=4; 4. a=1, b=5, c=4, d=3, e=2; 5. a=2, b=1, c=4, d=3, e=5; 6. a=3, b=5, c=1, d=4, e=2; 7. a=2, b=4, c=5, d=3, e=1; 8. a=5, b=1, c=2, d=4, e=3; 9. a=4, b=3, c=1, d=2, e=5.

Your credit card personality

Do you have your number? Okay, let's match it to one of the five credit card personalities. Find your personality type and get an idea of the right type of card for you. If you find that you're on the cusp between two personalities, then read both of the descriptions and look at the card suggestions. There isn't a quiz in the world that can *exactly* pinpoint your type. So use this as a guideline to help you proceed in the right direction.

After the personality section, you can read about each type of credit card, so you get a better understanding. There are some credit cards that have subcategories, like rewards cards. If this is your match, you have a smorgasbord of choices. Learning about the different types of rewards will help you pick the right type of rewards card for your lifestyle.

Your score is 9–14: Power User

I don't have to tell you that you're the boss of your credit cards because you already know that. You apply for and use cards strategically, you pay all of your credit card bills in full every month, and you always read the fine print.

You take your rewards very seriously. You could be either into miles or cash back, or both. You love to tell your friends about the free trips you take or how much cash back you got on your grocery expenses last month—or both.

Credit Status: Usually excellent, though it can dip into "good" territory if you're in the middle of an extreme credit maneuver. This could mean signing up for a credit card to get a free ticket or $200 cash. Or you could be engaged in a little credit card arbitrage. (If you're wondering what extreme credit is, don't worry. We will cover that in Chapter 11. Credit card arbitrage is an example of this extreme credit.)

Your credit card type: Rewards credit cards, charge cards, and if you're a small business owner, business cards.

Your score is 15–26: The Juggler

You carry a balance a few times a year. You're not heavily in debt, but cash flow often makes it difficult to pay the bill completely every month. You have to juggle your finances to make everything work but, most of the time, you're on top of things.

This personality often has an unpredictable income or simply doesn't have the cash to always make ends meet. But you're not living above your means intentionally. You're doing the best you can.

Credit Status: Jugglers can have excellent credit, if they're successful with the juggling act. As long as each ball stays in the air, they pay their bills and maintain a good credit score. They're not irresponsible, they're just not in a high-paying job and they have responsibilities, like kids or aging parents.

But if Jugglers start dropping balls and making late payments, then their credit status can plummet to good or fair. They don't have the ability to pay off debt quickly, so once interest starts compounding, it can get ugly. Be careful to keep those balances low and work on building an emergency fund in case your cash flow fails you one month.

Your credit card type: Low-interest credit cards. Stay away from rewards cards until you can successfully pay your balance off every month.

Your score is 27–33: The Rebuilder

For whatever reason, you find yourself in rebuilding mode. You probably have bad credit, but if so, you're working on it. You might be recovering from a bankruptcy or you have an account or two in collections. You're not feeling sorry for yourself, though. You're learning everything you can about credit so you can fix your life. At this point, the best thing to do is stay positive. Focus on the future and read Chapter 10, where I show you seven ways to rebuild your credit.

Credit Status: Rebuilders usually have poor or bad credit. It takes time to rebuild your credit history and improve your FICO score.

Your credit card type: Secured credit cards. There are unsecured cards for those who have bad credit, but you have to be careful to avoid predatory lenders. In most cases, a secured credit card can really help you rebuild your credit.

Your score is 34–42: The Accidental Debtor

You have serious debt, but there are extenuating circumstances. You may have gotten into debt due to an extended period of unemployment. Perhaps you or a family member became ill and the medical bills are destroying your cash flow and your emergency fund.

In spite of this, you usually pay your credit card bill on time. You take your credit score seriously so you pay the minimum and try not to max out your cards. You have cards with high credit limits, so your score hasn't been trashed. But you live in fear that you'll never pay off the debt.

Credit Status: Accidental debtors used to have good or excellent credit, and some of them still do. But they constantly worry their status will change if they can't keep up the payments. Many in this group are what the industry calls "fallen angels." They had great credit until unfortunate circumstances came into their lives.

Your credit card type: Balance transfer credit cards. These cards can be a life saver for folks who have good or excellent credit. They will give you a chance to pay down your debt—or pay it off completely—without paying interest for a period of time.

Your score is 43-plus: Walking Disaster

Even FEMA (the Federal Emergency Management Agency) can't fix the devastation you leave in your path following a trip to the mall. There are a couple of things going on here.

Sometimes, Walking Disasters are spending recklessly due to an emotional issue or due to a complete lack of money management skills. If Walking Disasters makes you think of *The Walking Dead*, it's kind of appropriate because, after a while, you definitely start feeling like you're in credit purgatory where you're stuck forever.

But sometimes, they're actually compulsive shoppers—true shopaholics—and they can't help themselves. This is the shopper who goes into DSW for a needed pair of running shoes, but exits the store with three pairs of shoes and a leather bag. Or, this is the shopper who has to have the latest in smartphones, no matter how much it costs. Or the shopper who goes to Lowe's to buy a new gas grill and comes home with the grill, plus new lawn furniture and shelving units for the garage.

Credit Status: Walking Disasters usually have fair, poor, or really bad credit. It depends on whether or not they've paid attention to due dates on their statements.

Your credit card type: Step away from the cards with your hands up so I can see them.

If your spendthrift ways are due to a lack of money management, you might be able to use cards after you pay off your debt. Personal finance skills can be developed as long as you're motivated to learn.

In some cases, even emotional issues can be resolved with therapy or new personal insights into why you feel the need to spend money. When I was a Walking Disaster, my issues involved a lack of money skills as well as a splash of emotional neediness. I grew up without money and then when I had it, I went crazy.

But if you feel you're a compulsive shopper, be honest with yourself. Credit cards are not for everyone. It's a horrible feeling to live with credit card debt. Don't be hard on yourself, either. We all have issues that we have to deal with.

Credit card types: what you need to know

I'm going to give some examples for each category because I think that will help you. But remember that terms change frequently in the credit card world, and these examples are just meant to help you understand the category.

If you're interested in a specific credit card I've used as an example, you can see a thoroughly neurotic review of the card on my Website, *BeverlyHarzog.com.*

Credit cards for the Power User

You'll learn in-depth details about rewards cards in Chapter 7, so this is just an overview of what's available on the market. The reason you need to be a Power User to use rewards cards is because they often have higher interest rates than non-rewards cards. This is because the credit card company has to cover their costs for giving you the rewards. So these cards are not recommended for anyone who carries a balance. The interest charges will wipe out your rewards.

Rewards credit cards can be broken down into several sub-categories. If you are a Power User personality, you can stick with one type of rewards card or mix and match to your heart's content. There are cash back, airline-branded cards, general travel rewards, and points.

Cash Back. These credit cards let you earn cash back rewards on purchases. The rewards programs vary quite a bit. For instance, you might have a card that offers 1 percent cash back across all of your purchases. Or your card might offer 2 percent in a specific category and then 1 percent on all other purchases. Here are a few examples that show how different these cards can be.

Often, you'll see an emphasis on everyday expenses. For instance, the American Express Blue Cash Everyday Card gives you 3 percent on groceries (with a cap of $6,000; then you get 1 percent), 2 percent in gas and department stores, and 1 percent on everything else. The Capital One Quicksilver Cash Rewards card gives you 1.5 percent on all purchases.

One of the most popular types of cash back cards are those with 5 percent bonus categories that rotate every quarter. These cards generally give 1 percent cash back on all purchases, but every quarter you'll get 5 percent cash back on chosen categories. For instance, you might get 5 percent cash back on gas purchases and dining. There's usually a cap, and after that, you get 1 percent on the category.

Redemption options sometimes include a good old-fashioned check with your earnings, a statement credit, or the opportunity to use your rewards for gift cards, travel, and lots more.

Airline-branded. These credit cards associated with a specific airline are called co-branded cards. For example, the Gold Delta SkyMiles Credit Card from American Express is a partnership between Delta and American Express. Delta markets the card and the rewards are targeted to consumers who fly Delta. It benefits both companies financially, but Delta also benefits from a branding standpoint. Every time you whip out your card, you see Delta's name.

Airline-branded cards are great for those who are loyal to one airline and who fly a lot. If you prefer to fly a variety of airlines, then a general rewards card would be a better choice. There are also hotel-branded cards, such as the Marriott Rewards Premier Credit Card. If you're loyal to a particular brand of hotels, these cards give you a chance to earn free hotel stays.

General tavel rewards. If you like flexibility when you travel, then you'll like travel rewards cards. Often, these cards give you the chance to transfer your points or miles to your choice of frequent flyer programs. There are several excellent cards in this category. For example, the Capital One Venture Rewards Credit Card offers two miles for every dollar spent. And you can use the miles on any airline.

As always with credit cards, few things are standard. The Chase Sapphire Preferred Card gives you two points per dollar spent on travel and dining. But you can increase the point value if you book your trip on Chase's Ultimate Rewards booking tool. So keep in mind that each credit card in the travel rewards category will have its own program rules, all the way down to seat restrictions or blackout days. But if choosing your own airline is important, a general travel rewards card is the way to go.

Points. It's sometimes difficult to decide which cards to put in which category. There's a little crossover between travel rewards and rewards points cards. I think of the rewards points cards as those for consumers who want to earn points quickly and then have a variety of redemption options. They might choose travel, but they want other options, too.

An example is the Citi ThankYou Preferred Card. You earn a point for every dollar spent and you get a vast array of choices for redemption options. You can redeem points for gift cards, merchandise, travel, and even get "Your Wish Fulfilled," which involves talking with a Wish Specialist and making one of your dreams come true, which is pretty darn cool if you ask me.

Business credit cards. If you're a small business owner, a business card can really help you run your business. You can choose a card with rewards and get some excellent rebates. These cards also often have cool management tools, such as custom reporting to track employee expenses.

You can choose the type of rewards that matches your expenses. For example, if you travel a lot, one option is the Capital One Spark Miles for Business credit card. You get two miles for every dollar spent. There are also business credit cards that offer cash back rewards.

Charge cards (consumer and business). The biggest difference between charge and credit cards is that a charge card balance has to be paid in full every month. So with charge cards, you think of them as a way to get a short-term (one month) interest-free loan that also gives you rewards. In fact, many charge cards also have excellent rewards programs. For instance, the American Express Gold Card is a charge card that lets you earn points you can redeem for travel, dining, and a whole lot more.

Credit cards for The Juggler: low interest

If you're a Juggler, low-interest credit cards are perfect for you because they minimize the interest expense you pay when you carry a balance. When I say "low interest" I mean the ongoing rate that you get is low. It's not just an introductory offer. Credit cards of all types sometimes offer a zero percent intro APR for a specified time period. But when the introductory period ends, the regular rate ends up being between 12 and 20 percent.

Even if you're not a Juggler, it's a good idea to have a low-interest credit card in your credit card stable. Why? They're great for those unexpected and expensive things that happen in life. Examples: Your fridge breaks down, your car needs new brakes, you need an appendectomy, your kid has a big growth spurt and needs new clothes for the next season, your dog needs surgery. (Okay, I'll stop.)

Now, true low-interest cards are often called plain vanilla cards. Their main feature is the low rate and they don't have rewards. But even standard cards come with a few nice benefits and perks. A good example of this type of card is the Simmons First VISA Platinum credit card. You get a 7.25 percent variable APR. The catch is that you need excellent credit to qualify, but if you've got the score, this is a great card to have if you carry a balance sometimes or to keep in your back pocket for those unexpected expenses.

The Rebuilder

If you're a Rebuilder, your options will depend a lot on *why* you're rebuilding. For instance, coming back from a bankruptcy is more challenging than coming back from late payments. So just keep that in mind. But for now, think about secured credit cards, and possibly retail cards, as tools to help you rebuild.

Secured credit cards. I really like these cards for establishing or rebuilding your credit. You make a deposit in a bank account and that becomes your collateral for the credit card. It "secures" the card for you.

You get a credit card that looks and works like all credit cards. The deposit stays in your bank account, so when you use the secured card, you really are buying things on credit. There are vast differences between the good cards and the very bad cards. I have a list of ranked cards on my Website and it's one of my most popular posts. The Capital One Secured MasterCard is an example of a popular secured card from a major bank.

Retail credit cards. Some stores offer their own credit cards. I'm not talking about retail rewards cards that offer a program where you earn some type of discount by making a certain amount of purchases at the store.

Some of these cards have sky-high interest rates, so you have to be cautious. But some of them aren't too bad. If it's a place where you shop regularly and you don't carry a balance, you can save money with these cards. Just be very careful to read the fine print.

These cards are all over the place. The Best Buy Reward Zone credit card has a variable APR of either 25.24 percent or 27.99 percent. On the other hand, The TrueEarnings Card from Costco and American Express has a variable APR of 15.24 percent.

The Accidental Debtor: balance transfer credit cards

These credit cards are designed to help you get out of credit card debt. You transfer your balance from a high-interest card to another card that has a zero percent introductory APR on balance transfers for a specified amount of time. This gives you a chance to pay off your balance while you pay zero interest.

Both Discover and Citi are known for their excellent balance transfer cards. And Chase often has a good offer on a few of its cards, too. If your credit score has dropped, a secured credit card might also be an option.

Credit cards for college students

If you're a college student, you have the option of applying for a card designed especially for students. Another option for students who don't have any credit history is secured cards, which I just reviewed in the previous section.

Student cards. These cards are designed to help college students build a credit history. And you do have to be enrolled in college to be considered for one of these cards. And yes, the issuer will confirm that!

The Credit CARD Act put new restrictions in place for issuing credit cards to individuals under 21. You have to show that you have the independent ability to repay debt, or have an adult co-signer who agrees to accept joint liability for the account.

A good example is the Discover It for Students credit card. The credit requirements for approval are a little bit looser than they are for the regular version of this card. Discover also has a student center that gives young consumers resources to learn more about responsible credit behavior.

How to compare credit cards

If you've never searched for and compared credit cards, the options can seem overwhelming. With the Internet at your fingertips, it's almost like an embarrassment of riches. Relax, though: I'll tell you the most efficient ways to find and compare cards. There's no one true way to do this. I'm going to give you the best search tips I know, and you can choose one or all of them to help you make a shortlist of credit card candidates.

On my Website, I do what I call "neurotically thorough" reviews. I spend about four hours on each card. I read the fine print, of course, but then I also scan the Internet for consumer reviews or any news that's relevant to the card. I also write my reviews in a somewhat folksy (sometimes snarky, if the card's so bad it makes me mad) style. I try to make it sound like we're having a conversation because I want you to make it through the reviews without wanting to stick a fork in your eye. Reading card reviews can be painfully dull. When I get e-mails from folks telling me they enjoy reading my reviews, I'm in heaven. That means I'm doing my job right!

When you get a shortlist of credit cards, I invite you to come to my Website and read my reviews of the cards. Feel free to ask me questions about any card. If you don't see a review for the card, ask me to write one for you. Think of me as the credit card version of a piano player in a bar. Your first stop is a credit card comparison Website. I have a few favorites, and here are my reviews of the sites.

Credit card comparison Websites

You need to know that sometimes you'll see credit cards placed in prominent areas and labeled something like "featured credit card" or "editor's pick." These issuers usually pay to have this title or to have a prime position on the page. The Websites aren't doing anything wrong. This is one of the ways Internet businesses make a living. I just want you to be aware of this practice, so you can ignore any special honors a card seems to have.

Here's a list of credit card comparison Websites for you to visit: LowCards.com (one of my favorite features is the sortable Card Index that lists more than 1,060 credit cards), CreditCards.com (the news articles on this Website are an example of top-notch journalism), NerdWallet (also has a huge database of credit cards), CardHub.com, Credit.com, CardRatings.com, and CreditDonkey.com (excellent graphics).

Google searches

You can always use Google to put your credit card list together. Be specific and type in what you're looking for. This will bring up credit card home pages, but you'll also see articles written about the type of cards you're looking for.

Don't fall for the "Best Card for Blah Blah Blah" spiel. I've written these myself, but these days I try to have a list of several cards of the best whatever. There is not a "Best Card" that's appropriate for every person in the United States. These lists don't take into account your credit card personality, for one thing. But do use these "best of" articles to find cards to research. The best card is the one that's best for you, not for the entire free world.

Read consumer reviews

I love reading consumer comments about specific cards. Some of my card reviews have gotten great feedback in the comments section. I also find good comments on the Credit Boards and on Credit Karma, too.

However, you can't read just one negative review and assume the card is bad. Don't take negative comments too seriously unless you see a pattern. Some people love to go on the Internet and complain, especially because they can do it anonymously. So read enough reviews from a variety of Websites to get a feel for what cardholders think. This is just one tool in your search arsenal.

You know about the different types of cards and you know how to put together a list of cards to review in detail. You're now ready to conquer the fine print. In the next chapter, you'll learn how to review the rates, fees, and other terms and conditions without swearing. If you find an outrageous fee, though, you're allowed to swear, but not in front of young children.

4

The Fine Print
Made Easy

D o you ever feel like you're reading a foreign language when
you try to read credit card agreements? It's all that legalese.
I mean, I understand why they write it the way they do. The
disclosure statements (the credit card agreement, terms and conditions, rewards programs, and so on) are written by lawyers and
their job is to protect the credit card company. These documents,
however, aren't written with consumers in mind.

Well, that's exactly why this chapter is in this book.
Consumers need a place to get a clear and concise explanation of things like "APR for Cash Advances." In a nutshell, this
chapter explains the fine print in a way that makes you feel
empowered instead of dazed and confused.

The credit card's home page
The major credit cards each have a home page and it's
loaded with information, all of which will be positive. This is
marketing, after all. It's no different from walking into a store
at the mall and seeing "Our Best Sale Ever" signs.

Still, you'll see an overview of the features, rates, and highlights of the rewards program. Think of it like buying a car. You see a model on the lot and you have an instant impression. Actually, that analogy isn't far off. Many people are attracted to a card because of the way it looks. Not that there's anything wrong with that. Just be sure that you don't judge the card on the pizzazz factor alone.

On the home page you'll also get the scoop on the sign-up bonus, if there is one. The bonus is usually an amount that you receive if you spend a certain amount within three months or so. If it's a card that fits within your lifestyle, you can use the card to buy things you were going to buy anyway. That way, you earn the extra cash without going over budget just to qualify for the bonus.

You might get a look at all the benefits and perks, but sometimes that requires digging. American Express goes to town with all this. They have great benefits and perks and they flaunt it. And you know what? They totally should. You want to know what a card offers so you can take advantage of the perk or benefit when you need it.

Terms: pricing, rates, and fees

Let's start with the Schumer Box. Don't be alarmed if you've never heard of this or have no idea what it's referring to. This is one of those terms that is tossed about in news articles or on cable TV, as if everyone chats about Schumer Boxes over coffee every morning.

Senator Charles (aka, Chuck) Schumer created the legislation that required terms of credit cards to be clearly displayed in marketing materials. It actually is a box as you can see on page 81. The law was enacted in 1988 and took effect in 1989. It also requires credit card companies to show long-term rate information in 18-point type and other significant disclosures in 12-point type. And thanks to the magic of the magnifying feature on our computers, you can make the dog-gone type as big as you want.

So where exactly is this box? I really wish I could give you a definite answer to this question. I've seen it at the top of pages, at the bottom, on the side, you name it. The best I can do is to say: Look for it. I've never seen it referred to online as the Schumer Box. Most often, you'll see something along the lines of "Terms and Conditions" or "Pricing and Terms." Keep clicking until you see it.

What you'll find in the Schumer Box

There are two sections in the box. I'll show you a list of what you'll find there and then I'll go over each element. And I promise, you won't want to throw yourself off a cliff before we're done. You'll start to feel empowered and in charge of your cards (pun intended).

Interest Rates/ Interest Charges	
Annual Percentage Rate (APR) for Purchases	0% introductory APR for 12 billing cycles from date of account opening. After that, your APR will be 11.99%, 16.99%, or 21.99% based upon your creditworthiness and will vary with the market based upon Prime Rate.
APR for Balance Transfers	0% introductory for 12 billing cycles from date of account opening. After that, your APR will be 11.99%, 16.99%, or 21.99% based upon your creditworthiness and will vary with the market based upon Prime Rate.
APR Cash Advances	24.99% This APR will vary with the market based on Prime Rate.
Penalty APR When It Applies	None.
How to Avoid Paying Interest on Purchases	Your due date is at least 25 days after the close of each billing cycle. We will not charge you interest on purchases if you pay your entire balance by the due date each month.

Minimum Finance Charge	None
For Credit Card Tips From the Federal Reserve Board	To learn more about factors to consider when applying for or using a credit card, visit the website of the Federal Reserve Board at www.consumerfinance.gov/learnmore

Fees	
Annual Fee	None

Transaction Fees
   Balance Transfer
   Cash Advance
   Foreign Transaction
	3% of the amount of each balance transfer
	4% of the amount of each cash advance
	3% of the amount of each transaction if there is no currency conversion

Penalty Fees
   Late Payment
   Over the Credit Limit
   Returned Payment
	Equal to the minimum payment due, but no more than $25
	NONE
	Up to $35

In the top section, "Interest Rates and Interest Charges," you'll see the following information:

- ◆ Annual percentage rate for purchases.
- ◆ APR for balance transfers.
- ◆ APR for cash advances.
- ◆ Penalty APR and when it applies.
- ◆ Paying interest.
- ◆ For credit card tips from the Consumer Financial Protection Bureau.

Annual percentage rate for purchases. The annual percentage rate (APR for short) reflects the *actual* cost of borrowing money for a year. So it's the interest rate plus any fees that are charged, for instance, an annual fee. A credit card usually has several APRs and the one for purchases is listed first.

Sometimes, for purchases, you'll see one APR. Whoever gets approved for the card gets this APR. Or you might see a set of two or three possible APRs. Another possibility is seeing an APR range. If there's more than one APR, you have to apply and get approved to know the exact rate. Here are some examples so you can see what I mean:

- Your APR on purchases will be 12.99 percent.
- Your APR on purchases will be 12.99 percent to 22.99 percent.
- Your APR on purchases will be 12.99 percent, 17.99 percent, or 22.9 percent.

There are other terms that might be mentioned in this section. You might see an introductory offer. If there's an introductory APR, you'll see it here, too. This is an offer of a reduced APR (often zero percent) for a specific period of time. For instance, you might get a zero percent introductory APR for the first 12 months (some might say billing cycle). After that, your APR will revert to the go-to rate, which is the APR for purchases.

Most credit cards these days have a variable APR. This means the rate will vary with the prime rate. The prime rate is an index that's used by banks to set the rate for their prime—or best—customers. Credit card issuers tie their own APRs to the prime rate. If the prime rate goes up, your rate goes up by the same amount of percentage points. If the prime rate goes down, your APR goes down too.

Annual percentage rate for balance transfers. This is the APR that's applied to balance transfers. Usually, consumers will decide to make a balance transfer to a credit card with a zero percent introductory APR. If there's an introductory offer, it will be shown here.

The APR for balance transfers is also almost always a variable rate that moves with the prime rate. If you have an introductory rate, you'll start paying the balance at the go-to purchase rate when the introductory rate ends.

Annual percentage rate for cash advances. This is the APR that's applied to cash advances and it's usually higher (sometimes much higher) than the purchase APR. That's the only thing you're told in the Schumer Box.

Here's the most important thing you need to know about cash advances: There's no grace period. The interest on a cash advance starts ticking right away. This little nugget is either mentioned in the section about paying interest or in an area below the Schumer Box.

Sometimes, there is an overdraft advance APR. Cash advances have credit limits, so if you exceed it, there's an APR for that. Just don't get a cash advance unless your life depends on it.

Penalty APR and when it applies. Pay attention to this number because it will give you incentive to pay your bill on time. It can be very high. Close to 30 percent isn't unusual. If it's triggered, it's your APR on new purchases. But if you're more than 60 days late, it can be applied to your entire outstanding balance.

This section will tell you what triggers the APR. For instance, the terms might say the penalty APR is applied if you make a late payment or your payment is returned. There will also be a mention of how long the rate will last. Usually, this will be vague and the issuer will say it will review your account periodically.

The CARD Act, which we talked about in Chapter 2, does state that issuers have to review your account and consider reinstating your old rate. However, it doesn't say they *have* to reinstate your old rate—just that they have to consider reinstating your old rate. If you end up in this situation, make sure you pay your bill on time for six consecutive months and then ask for a review if the issuer hasn't offered to give you one.

Paying interest. This is where you get information about your grace period. You'll be told that your due date is a specific number of days after each billing cycle closes. You won't have to pay any interest expense if you pay your balance in full during the grace period.

The grace period is generally between 21 and 25 days. The CARD Act requires credit card companies to mail your statement at least 21 days before the bill is due. Remember, as well, that business credit cards aren't protected by the CARD Act, so you might see a grace period less than 21 days. Keep in mind that not all credit cards have grace periods. The CARD Act put a time requirement on mailing statements *if* there was a grace period. There's no requirement that they have to have a grace period.

There are some credit cards, especially those targeted at consumers with bad credit, that start charging you interest as soon as it's posted to your account. I think this is predatory lending and I don't like it one bit. Now that you know where to find the grace period, if you're looking at a card that doesn't have one, then you need to choose another card. This is also where you might be told that interest starts accruing immediately on cash advances and balance transfers. Although I've seen this information below the Schumer Box, too.

Minimum interest charge. You won't always see this section, but right now, most of the major cards mention this in the Schumer Box. This is a short section and you're told what the minimum interest is if you have a balance, even a tiny one. This is often 50 cents or one dollar. But sometimes you'll see that there's no minimum.

For credit card tips from the Consumer Financial Protection Bureau. This has good intentions written all over it. You're told to visit the Website of the Consumer Financial Protection Bureau to learn more about the factors to consider when you apply for a credit card. The link provided just redirects you to information on the Federal Reserve's site and the FTC site. These Websites do have great information, but the original link is not hyperlinked, and the chances of someone copying and pasting it are pretty low.

Bottom section: Fees

The Penalty Fees section will vary a little. But generally, in the bottom section of the Schumer Box, you'll find the following:

- Annual fee.
- Transaction fees: Balance transfer, cash advances, foreign transactions.
- Penalty fees: Late payment, returned payment, returned check, over-the-credit-limit fees.

One thing I'd love to change about the Schumer Box is to have the rate and fee information for balance transfers in the same place. Instead, the APR is in the top section and the fee is in the bottom section. Now, they are separated in two different sections. This is also true for the cash advance APR and fee. If you see the balance transfer APR and don't see a transfer fee listed right there, you might assume that there's no fee. Be sure that you take the extra step to look for a transfer fee in the fees section of the Schumer Box.

Annual Fee

Not all cards have annual fees, but if they do, the amount will be listed here. Rewards cards often have annual fees, with the exception of some cash back cards. But souped-up versions of cash back cards, such as the Blue Cash Preferred, also tend to have annual fees.

If a card doesn't have a fee, you'll see "None." Even if the annual fee is waived for the first year, the amount is still listed so you know what you're liable for in the second year.

Transaction Fees

This is a very important section to review. Well, it's all important. But you need to know what the fees are before you even apply for a card. Don't be shocked when you're charged $125 for an annual fee because you didn't review it.

Balance transfer. The transfer fee is listed. The average is 3 percent, but some are as high as 5 percent. Once in a blue moon, an issuer will waive the transaction fee and also have a nice zero percent introductory rate. I can come up with a short list of issuers who waive the fee, but it's unusual when an issuer waives the fee *and* has a great introductory offer on balance transfers. At the time I'm writing this, there's exactly one such offer.

Cash advances. The transaction fee is listed here. The average is 3 percent, but some are as high as 5 percent.

Foreign transactions. These fees range from zero to 3 percent. A few credit card companies waive them entirely. Others waive these fees on their elite cards, but not across all of their cards.

Penalty Fees

This is my least favorite part of the Schumer Box. I have too many bad memories from practically living in this tiny rectangle of information. It's like the tiny box of shame. As far as the types of fees included here, I've done them all. Actually, the Schumer Box came into existence after I was already cleaning up my act. But because I didn't look at the fine print back in those days, it wouldn't have helped me anyway.

Late payment. This is usually around $35. Not all issuers will charge you a late fee or report you to the credit bureaus if you otherwise have a stellar record. But don't test it.

Returned payment. This can be up to $35. A returned payment can also trigger the penalty rate and cause you to lose the zero percent introductory rate.

Returned check. This can also be up to $35 and with the same situation as the returned payment.

Over-the-credit-limit fees. The CARD Act put the brakes on over-the-limit shenanigans. Banks were making lots of money on

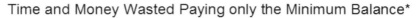

Time and Money Wasted Paying only the Minimum Balance*

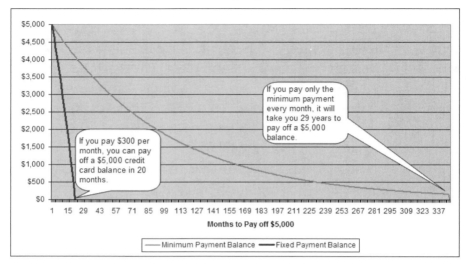

- If you have $5,000 in credit card debt and pay only the minimum balance it takes 29 years to pay it off and you spend $9,691 in interest on a $5,000 loan

- If you pay a fixed amount of $300 per month, you pay the loan off in 20 months and pay only $1,141 in interest

* Assumes a 24% interest rate and a requirement to pay 1% of the principal each month

these fees. Now, you have to opt in to be able to use your card even if you go over the limit. But in many cases, you'll get charged with a fee. The good news is that if you don't opt-in, your card will be denied. Isn't that better than spending more than you should?

Below the Schumer Box

This will vary by issuer and also by the type of card. Usually, there's an authorization section that informs you they'll be pulling your credit report. There also might be more detail about balance transfers, if there's an introductory offer with this card. You also get information about additional cards, replacement cards, how your balance is calculated, and what triggers the loss of your introductory

APR. There are also details about specific states and if the terms are different in those states.

One of the reasons you need to read it all is because when you apply for a card and start using it, you're accepting "the contract" for all the terms, conditions, rates, and fees. But if we're all honest, including the banks, it's a one-way contract. You agree to everything they say. And then they agree they can make changes to the rates and fees whenever they want (in accordance with the CARD Act rules). They can also change the rewards program at the drop of a hat.

How we will calculate your balance. The most common method is the "Average Daily Balance" method, and this might include or exclude new purchases.

If it includes new purchases, the balance is the sum of the outstanding balances for every day in the billing cycle (including new purchases and deducting payments and credits) divided by the number of days in the billing cycle.

Now, if it excludes new purchases, the balance is the sum of the outstanding balances for every day in the billing cycle (excluding new purchases and deducting payments and credits) divided by the number of days in the billing cycle.

Most of the cards I review include new purchases. That's too bad, because your finance charges are higher with this method. Here's an example:

Start-of-cycle balance: $2,000

New purchase day 10: $500

Payment on day 15: $100

Balance from 1st through 9th = daily balance is 2,000

$2,000 \times 9 =$ **18,000**

On day 10, new balance is 2500

2500×5 (days 10–14) = **12,500**

Payment on day 15, so balance = 2400 (2500 − 100)

Days 15–30, 16 total, 16 × 2400 = **38,400**

38,400 + 18,000 + 12,500 = 68,900 / 30 = $2,296.66 is your average daily balance

Interest: (days in billing cycle / 365) × APR × average daily balance

Let's say the APR is 10 percent (same as .10)

.0821917 × .10 = .821917 × 2297 = 1887.94 = $18.87 interest

Daily compound interest generates more finance charges. The bigger the balance means the bigger the expense. Take a look at the table on page 88 to see just how expensive compound interest can be when you carry a $5,000 balance over a long period of time. It's very difficult to get out of debt when you only pay the minimum amount due each month.

The Truth in Lending Act describes different methods for calculating finance charges, and the average daily balance is one of them. Credit cards are an example of "open-end" credit. Another example is a home equity credit line. You have an amount you can borrow, and you decide how much. You can pay the balance in full or pay a part of it.

Minimum payments

For all the hoopla about paying your monthly payment on time, most agreements don't include information about how the monthly payment is calculated. This is going to vary but, according to a CreditCards.com survey, it's about 1 to 2 percent of the principle amount plus finance charges and fees.

For instance, Chase charges the greater of the following: 2 percent of the balance, 1 percent plus of all interest and any fees, or a minimum of $10. There might be other rules if your balance is less than $25.

Balance transfer instructions. Please read this if you're doing a balance transfer. I'll get into more details about this in Chapter 9, but know the basics. You'll get instructions to continue making payments to your accounts.

Rewards information. You'll get highlights on the home page, but there's usually much more information on other pages. Some issuers will give the basic details in the area under the Schumer Box. But you often have to jump around the Web to find details about redemption options, rewards levels, and so on. Right now, don't worry about the details that aren't listed with the rest of the fine print. I cover rewards credit cards in detail in Chapter 7.

Payment allocation. This will be different on business cards, but for consumer cards you'll see a statement that describes how they apply payments up to your minimum payment due to lower APR balances first and then, generally, payments you make that exceed your minimum payment due will be applied to your highest rate balance first.

Other information. You'll probably see information describing billing rights, terms and conditions of offer, and more. I'm not going to bore you with every detail because it varies by card. But you do need to read it.

Common fees to watch out for

Some of these are easy to find, and some are worthy of the "fine print gotchas" term I like to use. These fees are lying like snakes in the tall grass of the fine print. But if you plow through it with the mentality of a weed whacker, you'll find them.

Seriously, one reason people get surprised by a $10 fee for a payment by phone is that it's boring to read this information and most people don't bother. That's what the banks are counting on. Show them that you're made of tough stuff and you can't be tricked.

It often takes me hours and hours to review a credit card that targets consumers who have bad credit. You might find any—or all—of the following fees when you read the disclosure statements for a card for bad credit: application fee (also known as a processing fee), paper statements, monthly maintenance fees, credit limit increase fees (no joke), and more.

Credit limits

You'll receive your credit limit after you get approved for the credit card. You'll see attempts online to tell you what to expect, but really, your credit limit is tied to the specifics of your credit report and the information on your application. Some credit card issuers do let you know what the *minimum* credit limit will be.

If you aren't happy with the limit you receive, call your issuer and request a higher limit. If it doesn't work, then give it six months. Be a perfect cardholder during that time and try again.

Product add-ons

Products add-ons are services that the issuer will try to sell you to protect you from the uncertainties of life. Common add-ons are payment protection insurance and identity theft protection.

Payment protection insurance, also called debt protection, is like the vampire of credit card add-ons. It won't go away no matter how many lawsuits are tossed around. Some issuers have withdrawn these services, but they're still out there and I want you to know how it works. Payment protection insurance is presented as insurance that will cover your minimum payments if you have a financial disaster and can't make your payments. The coverage varies. Some might say they'll defer your payments for two years or pay a death benefit.

The cost of these plans range from around 85 cents to $1.39 per $100 in your monthly balance. So if your balance is $2,000, and the plan charges you one dollar per $100, then you pay $20 ($1 × 20). If your balance stays about the same, you will have paid $240 in a year.

The problem is that these plans have loopholes and they often don't pay out when you file a claim. A 2011 report from the Government Accountability Office (GAO) showed that the nine largest credit card issuers earned $2.4 billion in payment protection fees. Only 21 percent of that resulted in financial benefit to consumers. Do you want to know how much of the revenue was profit for the issuers? A whopping 55 percent!

In recent years, credit card issuers have been reprimanded for pushing payment protection insurance. The Consumer Financial Protection Bureau (CFPB) and the Federal Deposit Insurance Corporation (FDIC) conducted an investigation into Discover's marketing practices. Discover ended up paying $214 million to settle the charges that they had used deceptive marketing techniques to get cardholders to agree to the protection plans over the phone. Capital One was also reprimanded and last year agreed to pay $210 million in penalties and restitution.

The payment protection insurance is a good example of the lengths banks will go to develop a new revenue stream. Don't get me wrong. I'm a capitalist and these banks are for-profit companies and they have a right to make money. But they can't do it in a deceptive manner that breaks the backs of the consumers who made them profitable in the first place. I like to call it responsible capitalism.

Next up: everything you need to know about your first credit card. Even if you're on your 19th credit card, still take a look, especially if you have older teens who may ask for a credit card soon.

5

Your First Credit Card: Build Credit, Stay Debt-Free

Would you believe that the first widely used credit card was invented because some guy left his wallet in his other pants? In 1950, a businessman named Frank McNamara was dining out with his wife in a New York City restaurant. When it came time to pay the bill, he was horrified to realize he didn't have his wallet. Yep, it was in his other pants.

Fortunately for Frank, his wife had the money to bail him out. He vowed that he'd never experience such embarrassment ever again. Remember: This is 1950 and your wife isn't supposed to bail you out, especially in a public place.

Fast forward one year. Frank has been busy making sure he never gets embarrassed again. He went back to the very same restaurant with his business partner, a guy named Ralph Schneider. (No word on where Frank's wife was that evening.) When they got the bill, Frank paid it with a small cardboard card. Today, that card is known as the Diner's Club Card, a multipurpose charge card.

That, ladies and gentlemen, is known as the First Supper. Okay, technically, it was a charge card, but it marks the first time that credit was extended to a cardholder. That's your credit card trivia lesson for today. Now let's get to the details of your first credit card.

Who is on the market for a first credit card?

Before you skip this chapter to go count the credit cards in your wallet, take a few minutes to look it over. There are some tidbits here that even a jaded credit card vet would appreciate.

For instance, do you know what happens behind the scenes when you make a purchase with your credit card? Most people don't. And although that might not be crucial to being an informed cardholder, it does help you understand what's at stake when cards add fees, for example. There are a lot of companies involved when you buy a new CD.

This is also an essential read for anyone who's the parent of a teen. Don't fall into the easy trap of getting a prepaid card. There are much better options than that. A plain debit card attached to a checking account is a better option than a prepaid card.

There are several different groups of consumers who might be on the lookout for their first credit card. Here are the usual suspects:

- College students.
- Young adults who aren't going to college and instead are already working full-time.
- Immigrants who need to establish a credit history in America.

Here's another group that doesn't get mentioned a lot: older consumers who have limited credit in their own name. I know many women who had a difficult time getting credit when their spouses died. This particular problem is generally associated with women, considering that traditional roles were in place until just a few decades ago.

Would you believe that women didn't have the right to own a credit card until 1974? The Equal Credit Opportunity Act was enacted to prohibit discrimination on the basis of a variety of factors, including gender, race, religion, and much more.

So it's not unusual for a woman who was in a traditional marriage to not have a credit card account. Being an authorized user helps (we'll get to that later), but it's not the same as having an established and excellent credit history that is in your own name.

I even know a few women who aren't that old and had this issue because they didn't realize that married couples don't share credit reports. There's no such thing as a joint credit history. This usually surprises people. So if you're a stay-at-home parent, male or female, be sure you get a credit card account in your own name. You need to have your own credit history and your own credit scores.

How credit cards work

I think it's helpful to have a mental picture of what goes on when you make a purchase with your credit card. Here's a condensed version of what happens when you hand over your credit card to buy a pair of boots at DSW. It's okay to buy the boots because they are on sale and you've budgeted for the purchase. I'll bet you thought I was going to condone random shoe shopping.

Before we review the transaction flow, however, let me explain something. Do you know that Visa and MasterCard are not issuers? They're just payment networks. It gets confusing because you always see the logo on your card.

Let's say Chase is your bank and that you're using your Chase Freedom Visa cash back card. The cast of characters:

- ◆ You.
- ◆ Chase, your credit card issuer.
- ◆ DSW, your favorite shoe store.
- ◆ Wells Fargo, DSW's bank.
- ◆ Visa, the payment network.

1. You purchase a pair of rich mahogany leather boots (they're on sale, okay?) and you hand over your Chase Freedom Visa credit card to the cashier.

2. The cashier swipes the card (or you tap it because it has a computer chip). The information on the strip (or in the chip) is sent to DSW's bank, Wells Fargo.

3. Wells Fargo submits the transaction to Chase for approval (called authentication). If you don't have room in your credit limit or your account isn't in good standing, your card could be declined.

4. If approved, Chase sends an authorization code to Wells Fargo. The shoe store gets reimbursed for the amount of the sale less a discount fee.

5. DSW's bank, Wells Fargo, submits the transaction to your credit card company, Chase, for payment via the card network, which, in this case, is Visa.

6. Chase pays Wells Fargo for the price of your boots, less an interchange fee via the Visa card network.

7. Chase sends you a statement that will include the amount you paid for your boots plus any other items you purchased during the current billing cycle.

8. You send your payment for the full amount reflected on your balance to Chase.

You look awesome in your new boots. Your credit score is intact because you paid on time and have a low utilization ratio. The whole world is happy.

Young adults and the Credit CARD Act of 2009

You got a dose of the highlights of the CARD Act in Chapter 2. When the CARD Act was being written, one of the goals was to protect young adults. In fact, there's an entire section of the CARD Act called "Protection of Young Consumers."

Before the CARD Act, it wasn't unusual for credit card issuers to set up on campuses and offer students free pizza, mugs, and T-shirts to get them interested in applying for a credit card. Now, they can't offer gifts and freebies within 1,000 feet of campus.

From the student's perspective, though, having a credit card sounds like a lot of fun times ahead. They can get pizza at midnight whether they have the cash or not, and they can invite the whole dorm! For the kids who had been taught how to manage money and credit by their parents or some other caring person in their lives, they might be okay. But the truth is that most kids hit the college scene with very few money smarts.

The recent survey by mutual fund company T. Rowe Price showed that although parents think they encourage their kids to talk to them about money, only 19 percent of kids agree that's the case.

Proof of income

There was a time a decade or so ago when you could get a credit card if you could fog a mirror. In 2004, a little pug named Clifford, who lived in California, received a credit card offer. Clifford's owner filled out the application the way Clifford would have and, even though he made it clear on the form that this was a joke, Clifford got a credit card with a $1,500 limit.

Can you imagine if that happened in today's social media environment? Clifford would have his own Twitter account and tweet about the new chew toys he was buying on credit. These days, things like that don't happen very often because scrutiny is much tighter.

So the CARD Act decided to make it more difficult for a college student to get a credit card. Unfortunately, some students were listing their student loans as income and getting cards based on this.

I worked my way through college, so I know it's difficult to pay for everything. But really, the last thing you need is credit card debt on top of student loan debt. According to a survey by Sallie Mae, the average credit card debt for a college senior in 2009 was $4,100. The bottom line is that if you're under 21 and you don't have sufficient income, you can only get a credit card if you have a cosigner.

For a while, there was an uproar over the fact that stay-at-home spouses could no longer qualify for cards because they lacked independent income. In May 2013, the CFPB clarified the law and said that stay-at-home spouses or partners who are 21 years old or older can get access to credit cards as long as they can show they have access to household income.

Protection from prescreened offers

Everyone thought this meant that card issuers couldn't mail credit card offers to anyone under the age of 21. The law says that if you're under 21 you can opt in with the credit bureaus to have your name on a list. But even if you haven't opted in, kids sign up for things all over the Internet. So their names get on lists. It can be as simple as having a frequent flyer account or signing up for a rewards program.

This law may have made it more difficult to reach the under-21 crowd, but they're still getting offers and it's all done legally.

Strategies for establishing good credit

I like a holistic approach to credit. What I mean by that is you'll have more success managing your credit life (and avoiding credit card debt) if you learn the basics of personal finance. If you don't get the big picture, it's kind of like studying for a test that covers Chapters 1–5, but you only learned Chapter 4.

I didn't truly master my credit life until I understood budgeting, cash flow, savings accounts, basics of investing, and the art of finding bargains. Listen, this isn't difficult. You've got a world of information right at your fingertips on the Internet. Or go to your local bookstore (if you can still find one!) and settle down in a comfy chair with a stack of books. And on my Website, you'll find a list of personal finance books that can help you create the financial life you've always wanted.

It might be seem ironic, but the strategies for establishing credit are eerily similar to the strategies for rebuilding credit. You do have an advantage when you're starting out, though. You haven't done anything to screw up your credit, so the card issuer doesn't have a negative feeling about you from the get-go. (I will discuss the rebuilding strategies in detail in Chapter 10, where you'll pick up more useful tips that will help you understand your credit life.) Are you ready to be on your way to a fabulous credit history? Let's do this thing.

You can't build credit without using your credit card

A lot of people think that it shows restraint if you have credit and don't use it at all. They think this will be rewarded by the FICO score. That would be no. Though you are rewarded for keeping low balances, you do have to use your card to *generate* a score. Sometimes I like to joke that when it comes to credit scores, if it makes sense, it's probably wrong!

I talked about generating a score in more detail in Chapter 2, but here's a recap to refresh your memory. Your credit report must have an account that's been open for a minimum of six months, an undisputed account that has been reported to a credit bureau within the past six months, and there should be no indication that you're actually dead.

I don't know why that last one cracks me up, but it does. Anyway, if your goal right now is to build a credit history, use your card for small purchases and pay it off during the grace period. In about six months, you should start generating a score. Oh, and don't hang out with dead people.

Start with only one credit card. You need time to get used to tracking your expenses, making payments on time, and so on. Do not go on an application frenzy. Trust me: When you're green, you don't need a lot of credit.

Unsecured credit cards for zero or limited credit

If you have a full-time job and haven't accumulated any black marks on your credit history, you might have some decent unsecured options. You might even be getting these in the mail. Be careful that you don't apply for an unsecured credit card that's designed for folks with bad credit. Your situation is different. You have zero or limited credit, not bad credit. So if you get approached by First Premier Bank or Continental Finance, don't pursue it. Both of these issuers target the bad credit market, and their cards have high APRs and lots of fees.

If you come across Continental Finance's credit cards, The Matrix or The Cerulean, stay away. These cards have the Discover logo on them, but they are not issued by Discover. Discover is the payment network that's used to process credit card transactions. Many have been confused about this and thought they were signing up for a Discover card. Discover has excellent customer service (excluding the payment protection insurance fiasco), so many consumers were quickly disappointed when they realized they hadn't gotten a Discover card.

If you're a student, you have the option of applying for an unsecured student card from a major issuer. But if you're not a student or you just don't want a student card, here's what I suggest:

- Take a look at Capital One credit cards that target the average credit market. Currently, Cap One has several cards that are for consumers with average credit: Classic Platinum, Platinum, and Quicksilver One Cash Rewards.
- Try your local bank. Often, local banks will be willing to take a chance on you, especially if you have a checking or savings account with the bank.

◆ Credit unions often have terrific cards. You'll need excellent credit before you can get some of the popular cards, but try a local credit union. Again, if you're a customer already, it might help your case.

◆ Depending on the specifics of your credit report, you might have a chance to get an American Express Green Card. This is a charge card, not a credit card. But this can help you build credit.

Also, try networking the way you do when you're looking for a job. Find out what cards your friends have. It might not be the perfect card for you, but do some research and find out. If someone else who has limited credit has the card, then this is a sign that the issuer might be willing to take chances on young people.

Prepaid cards do not help you build credit

I'm not a fan of prepaid cards because the majority of them have so many fees. I think it's crazy to pay to spend your own money.

In my opinion, prepaid cards are for people who can't get a checking account. If you're in the Chex system, then I know you've got a problem. But even in this situation, view a prepaid card as a temporary solution. Work to get back into the traditional banking system so you can build credit. The Bluebird prepaid card from American Express and Wal-Mart is a decent option if you must use a prepaid card.

Remember this: *You cannot build credit with a prepaid card.* This confuses many people because they see a MasterCard, Visa, or an American Express logo on the card. That's just the payment network that the issuer uses.

You're using your own money when you use a prepaid card so you aren't buying anything on credit. Your payment history doesn't get reported to the major bureaus. To build your credit history, stick with a credit card and pay all of your bills on time.

Student credit cards

If you have a little bit of credit, you might qualify for student credit cards. What I like about these cards is that the issuers often have excellent credit education on their Websites. And the education is targeted to young Americans. For instance, the Discover Student Center is a very good resource. Capital One issues the Journey Student rewards credit card and also has a nice education center for students.

Now, the interest rates are on the high side unless you already have a good credit history. But this shouldn't matter because you're going to pay your bill off every month, right? (Okay, just checking.)

But the underwriting—basically, what they consider when approving you—is a little more forgiving for students. But you do have to be enrolled in a college or university to qualify for a student card. An executive at Discover told me that they do confirm if you're currently enrolled.

Secured credit cards

I will talk more about this in Chapter 10 because this is an excellent tool for rebuilding your credit. But if you find you can't get approved for an unsecured credit card, then this is also a good option for someone who's establishing their credit history.

Here's the gist of it: You make a deposit into a bank account and that "secures" the card for you. You then receive a credit card and it looks like any other credit card. And it also works like any other card.

Some financial Websites incorrectly call these prepaid credit cards. You are not using the deposited funds that are in your account. You're actually using a credit card and buying items on credit. As long as you choose a secured card that reports to all three major credit bureaus, you'll be able to use the card to build credit.

To help you choose the best card you can qualify for, I have a best-to-worst list on my Website of more than 20 secured credit cards. Each secured card on the list is also linked to one of my neurotically thorough card reviews. As well, if you have a parent or spouse in the military, there are some truly excellent secured cards available to you.

Become an authorized user

A while back, something called "tradeline renting" became a problem. This is a practice where a consumer with excellent credit takes money to allow a stranger to become an authorized user on his or her credit card account. A more common term for this is "piggybacking." Who thinks up all these devious ways to get ahead without having to do the work? Really, I can't imagine spending time thinking about how I can circumvent FICO scoring.

Apparently, however, some folks have too much time on their hands and very little sense, so this was a big problem. In 2009, the FICO 08 score was introduced to combat this problem. Originally, the score was going to ignore authorized user accounts. FICO changed the score, though, after there was a backlash from consumer advocates.

Thus, FICO 08 was changed so it included authorized user accounts, but FICO says the algorithm is supposed to be able to tell the difference between legitimate authorized users and the piggybackers. The bottom line is that you have no idea which FICO score your lender will use. And even if it's FICO 08, if you're a legitimate authorized user, which means you're connected to the account holder in some way, you'll get a benefit from being an authorized user.

If you're a piggybacker, you'll be found out and you won't benefit. There's talk that FICO 08 is being used frequently by lenders. Well, you know what? It doesn't matter to you. You know what you need to do to protect and boost your score. Responsible behavior takes care of your credit score, no matter which version they use.

If you decide to go the authorized user route, choose someone who is responsible and who has a very good credit history. And be sure you do your part and use the card responsibly. Be clear that you'll cover your charges and determine how you'll handle the logistics of paying back the cardholder.

As an authorized user, you are not legally liable for any credit card debt that ends up on this account. If the account owner suddenly defaulted, you would not be legally responsible for the debt.

Get a cosigner for an unsecured credit card

This isn't always an option because some cards don't allow you to get a credit card unless you can qualify on your own. There are some student cards with that requirement. Citi, as of this writing, does not allow cosigners on student cards. But for credit cards where it is an option, this can be an effective way to build your credit history.

Honestly, this can be a bit of a sticky wicket. From a legal standpoint, you're both liable for any debt on the card. If there's a late payment or worse, you both end up getting your credit scores trashed.

So be sure you know the individual is responsible and trustworthy. I hate to say this, but I've seen parents mess up their kid's credit this way and, of course, vice versa. I've also seen it work when the parent has great credit and pays close attention to everything the child spends money on. It can be time consuming, so consider that as well if you're the one doing the cosigning. If the parties involved do a great job of behaving responsibly, this is a good strategy to build your credit history. But proceed with caution.

Alternative credit

When you're building credit you've got that chicken or egg dilemma: How do you get credit if you don't have credit? If you don't have credit how do you get credit? It's frustrating.

If you have access to someone who will let you become an authorized user, that's a nice opportunity you can take advantage of.

But there are lots of folks out there, especially immigrants, who don't have that option.

If you feel like you've pursued the traditional avenues to credit and you've come up empty, consider alternative credit. There are many payments you make that aren't reported to the major credit bureaus. For instance, maybe you pay rent to your landlord, pay for utilities, pay for your cell phone, and pay for insurance.

You aren't making payments to these providers because you bought things on credit. So these types of payments aren't reported to the Big Three: Equifax, TransUnion, and Experian. Therefore, any payments that aren't considered for your credit report are considered "alternative credit."

Now, eCredable.com is a company that helps people who have no credit or what's called a "thin file" or limited credit. This company offers the eCredable AMP Credit Report. AMP stands for All My Payments. You do have to become a member to use this report, and it isn't free. You can take the report with you when you go to the bank to ask for a credit card, or when you visit an apartment and you want to show that you pay your bills responsibly.

When you show it to a creditor, the creditor is required by federal law to consider the information on your AMP Credit Report. The creditor is *not* required to give you the loan, though. This may or may not work out for you, but it's another option.

6

Plain Vanilla
Credit Cards

Rewards credit cards are sexy. Well, let me rephrase that. If there's *anything* sexy about credit cards, it's the rewards. Maybe it's the thought of what you can do with the rewards. You can travel to exotic islands with the miles you've accumulated. Use your points for an "experience" like a hot-air balloon ride or a chance to ride with a fighter pilot. And usually, rewards credit cards have a glamorous, glossy look.

If your Credit Card Personality Quiz results showed that you're a Juggler, which means you often carry a balance, you need to avoid rewards credit cards. The APRs on rewards credit cards tend to be high, so if you carry a balance, you'll just wipe out your rewards and maybe end up in debt, too.

I'm not condoning carrying a balance, of course. You know I preach the opposite. But we're talking about *real life* here. And sometimes real life gets awful messy. So it's good to have a low-interest credit card in place so you can minimize the financial damage to your life.

But even if you're a Power User, it's a good idea to have a low-interest credit card in your wallet. You just never know when you'll have an expensive emergency. With a low-interest card, you can carry a balance in an emergency situation for a few months and you should be okay.

Not your father's (or mother's) plain vanilla card

So what's a plain vanilla card? Basically, it's a credit card that doesn't have rewards. In the past, these cards were pretty bland. But nowadays, they have a lot more flavor. There was a time when plain vanilla credit cards used to be considered the card you'd get if you couldn't get approved for a rewards card.

Two things have changed over the years. The plain vanilla card isn't so plain anymore. They don't have rewards, but they have many extras that give the cards great value. The second change is that consumers no longer consider these basic cards to be a consolation prize. Consumers now understand that choosing a card without rewards but that has a low APR is a strategic move that makes a lot of sense.

The issuers know this and they've been pushing the plain vanilla cards again over the past two years. Mintel Comperemedia is a firm that tracks credit card industry information, including direct mailings sent out by credit card companies. In the spring of 2012, Mintel found that direct mail offers for the plain vanilla credit cards were pouring into consumers' mailboxes. Direct mail for credit cards with no rewards—and no annual fees—made up 30 percent of all the mailed offers during the last quarter of 2011.

Overall, the direct mailings for credit cards for 2012 were still lower than the mailings in 2011. According to Mintel, this can be partly explained by issuers using different avenues to reach consumers. Social media, such as Facebook, has become a significant marketing tool for card issuers. American Express, for example, has 2.7 million "likes" on its Facebook page.

But the uptick in the plain vanilla mailings told me that credit card issuers were turning their attention toward the consumer who values simplicity and low interest rates over rewards. Do you remember the term "credit crunch"? During the recession, that was one of the most overused terms. But it did describe a situation that many identified with.

Rewards cards are still extremely popular, no doubt. But I think consumers emerged from the recession a little more street smart when it comes to credit cards. Many had balances—and some still do—because they lost jobs or needed to use credit cards to meet monthly expenses.

But in all the decades I've been a finance writer, I've never seen the media have such intense coverage about credit. Partly, this scrutiny was because the mortgage debacle was front and center as one of the causes of the recession. However, many consumers also had credit card debt as a result of living beyond their means. I think these folks developed a better understanding of how to stay out of trouble with their credit cards. And having a credit card that has a low interest rate is a good way to stay out of trouble.

Why some people prefer plain vanilla cards

These cards actually have a lot of variety when it comes to the perks and features, even without the rewards programs.

Here are some examples of what is considered a plain vanilla card: Citi Simplicity, Chase Slate, PenFed Promise, and Simmons First Visa Platinum. Of these, the Simmons First and the PenFed Promise card are more like the plain vanilla cards of old. That isn't a criticism, just an observation. The Simmons First card and the PenFed Promise card both boast an extremely low APR.

The appeal of low interest rates

If you're a Juggler and you sometimes carry a balance, you absolutely have to have a credit card with a low APR. The lower the

APR, the less interest you'll pay. It all makes sense. Another reason that we just touched on is that it's nice to have an emergency card. Let me be clear, though: A credit card is a lousy replacement for a rainy day fund.

I'm going to come right out and ask you a nosy question: Do you have an emergency fund? It's okay; you can be honest. I'm the last person who would judge you. Remember: I'm the one who went on a cruise to Mexico and spent all but my last dime. I did have a fabulous time, but that's not the point.

The reason I'm asking about your rainy day status is because if you don't have one, you need to get busy with that. A low-interest card is great for a backup, but that shouldn't be your main source of funds when you need a new engine for your Toyota. A low-interest credit card can help you out if you don't have the $2,000 to fix your car. But if you also have an emergency fund, you can pay it off faster and save yourself some money.

So how low of an APR can you get? It all depends on the economic environment. Right now, if you have excellent credit, you might be able to get rates less than 10 percent; maybe even less than 8 percent. But for many consumers who have good-to-excellent credit, you're looking at closer to 12 percent and higher.

I've already talked about how some cards can have a range of APRs or just one low APR. The Simmons First Visa Platinum credit card has a variable 7.25 percent APR. (I'm not kidding.) Now, you need truly excellent credit to get that. But you can see how a low-interest rate can be a God-send if you don't have a rainy day fund.

Other cards in this category might offer a range or three different APRs so they can approve more folks and not just the consumers with a 750 FICO score. The riskier the credit profile, the higher the APR the bank will charge. This is classic CYA from a bank's point of view.

The Citi Simplicity card, for instance, offers three rates: 12.99 percent, 17.99 percent, or 21.99 percent, based on your creditworthiness. That means they'll decide which APR you'll get after they review your credit report and assess how risky you might be as a cardholder.

If you have excellent credit, you're most likely looking at 12.99 percent. But if you don't have excellent credit, the APR can get high in a hurry. Once your rate gets into the mid-teens and up, it's not really a good card for revolving a balance or for an emergency. The exception is that the emergency is of a very short-term nature.

If there are unexpected circumstances in your life that make cash flow an issue, then that's an unfortunate fact. But if it's something you can change, I urge you to do so because I want you to be debt-free and never pay interest expense.

No annual fees

Most plain vanilla cards don't have annual fees. Rewards credit cards usually have them because they offer rewards. The annual fees help the bank offset the loss of revenue.

With rewards cards that offer very generous rewards and perks, the annual fees can get high. Hundreds of dollars isn't uncommon for the elite cards. But if you're in the market for a plain card, you're not interested in the rewards or the chance for priority boarding.

On the other end of the credit card spectrum, credit cards for bad credit and secured credit cards usually come with annual fees, too. This is because the issuers feel the need to offset the risk of the cardholder.

No-frills cards are easier to understand

If you've ever tried to get through a credit card's rewards program details, you can appreciate the concept of simplicity. Seriously, I sometimes have to go to three or four different Websites to get all the rewards details I need to properly review a card. I save every credit card offer that comes in my mailbox and see if there are more documents than what I found online.

I'm never really sure if I've read everything there is to read about a card. There just isn't a master list of disclosure statements for a card that I can check off as I read them. (Come to think of it, that kind of list would be a great thing to have.)

I think a standard, no-frills credit card is perfect for someone who's new to credit and who doesn't have a strong background in personal finance. Really, even a plain vanilla card has enough disclosure statements to make you want to consider a cash-only lifestyle.

Next we're going to talk about how plain vanilla cards have changed. Rewards credit cards might be the chocolate almond fudge version of credit cards. But now you can get toppings on your scoop of vanilla. The added features do add a touch of complexity, but the perks and benefits are worth it.

Common benefits (I'll take my credit card with sprinkles, please)

Even if you don't get rewards, you can benefit and sometimes even save money with the sprinkles—I mean, the benefits and perks. Most people never get full value from their credit card because they have no idea what their benefits are.

I'm not scolding you at all. The credit card companies don't make it easy for you to figure out how to take advantage of your benefits. It's almost as if they don't want you to know about them. I'm going to cover the most common benefits here, because you usually have these on rewards cards, too. So it's information you need to know.

What does platinum mean?

I don't spend much time worrying about standard, platinum, and gold categories. Issuers do have cards with these labels but, these days, individual cards can have a vast array of features. The credit company can make its own decisions about the benefits on its cards.

For example, a MasterCard platinum card offers certain benefits, but the card issuer has the final say about what actual benefits are offered to the cardholder. Platinum cards do tend to have higher credit limits than many of the standard plain vanilla cards. And gold cards have a higher credit limit than platinum cards. But I suggest you focus on the card and the specific benefits given by the issuer. Don't worry about possibly out-dated card definitions.

Zero percent APR introductory offers

You learned about zero percent introductory rates in Chapter 4. There are exceptions, but you often find the longest introductory rates with the basic cards. I'm talking about zero percent rates on *both* purchases and balance transfers.

One exception, for example, is the Discover it Card. This card was just introduced in the past year as a replacement for its long-running Discover More card. It usually has a pretty good zero percent introductory offer on balance transfers and it's a good rewards credit card. I often recommend this card if a consumer wants to transfer a balance, pay off debt, and then have a rewards card when it's all said and done. Discover has been known as a good balance transfer card for quite a while.

Another basic card, the Chase Slate credit card, has had a limited time offer to waive the transaction fee on balance transfers. In the past few years, I've seen credit cards waive the fee a number of times. There are some cards out there that don't charge balance transfer fees at all, but they typically don't come with zero percent introductory offers. The interest-free period is the most important part.

Even if there aren't any cards waiving transaction fees when you buy this book, just hang tight. Check with my blog (*www.beverlyharzog.com/my-blog/*) because I'm always staying on top of trends and I can tell you if there are new offers on the market. These things are cyclical, similar to the economy.

Amped-up customer service

Who doesn't enjoy special attention? Personally, I love a good concierge service. Some of the elite cards (with annual fees) come with this, but it's possible to find them in basic cards as well.

The Citi Diamond Preferred, for instance, offers 24/7 concierge service and will help you book hotels and flights. Plus, there's a Citi Private Pass service that helps cardholders get preferred tickets to concerts and other events. I love sports, especially baseball, so I'd love to have help getting preferred tickets.

So does the word "preferred" change it from no-frills to premium? Not in my view. It doesn't offer rewards and the APR starts as low as 11.99 percent. The concierge service is a cherry on top. It's a topping, like sprinkles.

And while some other vanilla cards don't offer a concierge service, they might offer 24/7 access to customer service. This is a great feature if you're experiencing a financial emergency. You never know when you're going to need some help.

Travel perks

You might not get travel rewards, per se, but you might get some travel-related benefits that offer great value. Remember the Simmons First card with the 7.25 percent APR? It comes with travel accident insurance to the tune of $1,000,000. That card also comes with other travel-related perks, including car rental loss/damage waiver, and help when you need emergency cash or a credit card replacement. Other travel-related perks on some of the basic cards include lost luggage coverage, medical assistance, legal referrals, and emergency roadside assistance.

One of the most inconvenient things to happen, especially if you're already sitting at the gate, is to have your trip canceled.

Once, when my kids were small, we planned a Key Largo/Disney vacation. After a few days of snorkeling and boating in Key Largo, we drove to the Miami airport where we were scheduled to fly to Orlando for the Disney part of our vacation.

Well, guess what? Our plane had been struck by lightning during the night before our flight. So, yes, the plane was grounded and so were we. Rather than spend 12 hours waiting for the next flight, we rented a car and drove to Orlando.

This was during a time when I was just getting back into credit cards and I didn't really understand all the travel perks my card had. I feel sure, though, that I probably could have saved some money. At least we did have the presence of mind to use a rewards card to pay for the rental and the gas.

Before a trip, always take a look at your card's policies because you might even have coverage for canceled trips. For example, some Citi cards have trip cancellation/interruption coverage of up to $1,500.

Auto rental insurance

This can certainly save you money. But you have to take it upon yourself to read up on the benefits for your particular card. In general, your credit card's insurance is your secondary insurer if you have primary auto insurance. And unless you live in a place where you don't need a car, you probably have car insurance.

Another important point to remember is that you must use your credit card to rent the car for the insurance to apply. That might seem obvious, but you can see how many might think that you're covered because you're a cardholder.

The level of coverage varies a lot by payment network (Visa, MasterCard, Discover, and American Express) and by issuer. For instance, credit cards issued by Chase and that use the Visa payment network might still vary by card. So, sorry, but the only way to know your benefits is to read the fine print. If it isn't clear to you, call your issuer and ask for an explanation.

Purchase-related benefits

I'd have to say that American Express cards are tough to beat in this category. You really get excellent protection. But most cards offer one or more of the following:

- ◆ Extended warranty: The original manufacturer's U.S. warranty is often extended by a certain amount, such as one year.
- ◆ Retail purchase protection: protection against fire, theft, or accidental breakage. Coverage has a cap and a time limit from the date of purchase.
- ◆ Zero liability on unauthorized purchases.

Recent trends in benefits and perks

I'm seeing a lot of unique perks being offered these days. They seem geared toward helping consumers manage their money more effectively. As long as this doesn't somehow end up raising rates or creating fees, I like it. (Do I sound a little jaded? Hey, it comes with the territory!) Let's look at some examples of the features and benefits that are designed to help consumers.

The new "no one's perfect" approach

The Citi Simplicity came out a few years ago with this feature. You can probably remember one of its commercials where a young makeup artist was on a faraway island and she hadn't paid her bill. Oh, and as luck would have it, they had to stay longer and reshoot scenes.

But she's saved because her Citi Simplicity card had her back. She won't be charged a late fee or get a penalty rate. Yay! Unfortunately, there's no word about whether her credit score got dinged for making a late payment. Last year, the Discover it Card was introduced with a similar concept. You're forgiven for your first late payment.

Another new card in 2012 was the BankAmericard Better Balance Rewards credit card. This card takes a different route to the "no one's perfect" approach. You can earn cash by paying more than the minimum on your balance. They have "rewards" in the card name, but I don't consider this a rewards card. If you're carrying a balance, you're not making a profit on your card.

We can argue all day long about the real intent behind these "helpful" cards (profit for the banks), but the fact is that these cards are designed for the way some consumers are handling them these days. Whether or not the bank profits from the cards isn't my main concern, to be honest. My concern is whether or not the card actually helps *you*.

So if you're in a spot where life isn't great at the moment and you're carrying a balance, then a credit card with a sympathetic approach may be right for you at this time. Just remember: There's no such thing as a free lunch. If you take advantage of opportunities to pay late or to get a bonus from paying more than the minimum, it will end up biting you in the you-know-what sooner or later.

Money management help

A great example of the trend to help you manage your budget is Chase's Blueprint. This is a free set of tools to help you manage your borrowing and spending. You can set up your Blueprint "plan" and track your progress online and on every statement. There are four plans to choose from:

- Full pay: avoid interest even when carrying a balance.
- Split: create a plan to pay off larger purchases.
- Finish it: pay down balances more quickly.
- Track it: look at your spending patterns.

If you got this card because you know you'll carry a balance, you get to choose which categories you'll pay in full each month. So even if you carry a balance, you won't pay interest on the categories you've chosen to pay in full. Of course, it's always better to pay your entire balance every month, but if you *must* carry a balance, it's cool to have control over how you allocate your payment.

One of the appeals of business credit cards is that they come with great tools to manage your credit. I think that approach is starting to cross over into the consumer segment of the credit card market. But, as in all things, if you really want to take advantage of money management tools, you have to put in the time to learn the features.

Bottom line

This chapter shows just a smattering of the types of perks and benefits you get with credit cards. But this varies a great deal by credit card. Also, remember that credit cards from the same issuer (for example, you have two cards from Chase) may have different benefits.

There's no shortcut here, I'm afraid. You have to read all of the disclosure statements to know what benefits and perks come with your cards. I gave you an overview so you'd have an idea of what types of benefits are out there these days, even if you don't have a rewards card.

Actually, many of the benefits I covered in this chapter will also be available on rewards cards. The trends, however, such as forgiving you for a late payment, will not. Rewards cards have their own trends and we'll get to that in the next chapter.

7

Rewards Credit Cards for Fun and Profit

How would you like to get a $352 airline ticket for $5? Last summer, I decided that I wanted to go to the Finance Bloggers Conference in Denver, which was scheduled for September 2012. I live in Atlanta, so I knew it wasn't going to be cheap. The cost of the ticket was $352, but I got it for the paltry sum of $5.

Here's how I did it: I needed a new travel rewards card anyway, so I picked a card that had a nice sign-up bonus and that would also be a great fit for my travel needs going forward. I could earn a sign-up bonus of 30,000 miles if I spent $500 within the first three months.

I reached the $500 requirement easily by using the card while we were on vacation. When I booked my flight to Denver, I redeemed my 30,000 miles, which had a redemption value of $300. I was able to cover the $52 with frequent flyer miles I already had. There was a $5 tax and that was what I paid for my round-trip flight to Denver.

What I did here was actually simple. Rewards cards are popular because, if chosen carefully, you can truly benefit just by going about your business. According to the Federal Reserve Bank of Boston, about 60 percent of consumers have a rewards credit card.

There are many different kinds of rewards credit cards, which are also referred to as premium credit cards. It's kind of hard to classify them because some cards fall into more than one category. Here's a list of the cards you're going to learn about in this chapter:

- ◆ Cash back cards.
- ◆ Co-branded, store, or retail cards.
- ◆ Travel rewards cards.
- ◆ Airline-branded and hotel-branded cards.
- ◆ General points and charge cards.

I'll go over each type of rewards card and give you an example or two of each card. Then we're jumping right into the rewards: Fine Print Boot Camp. Hey, stay right there! It's not painful at all. Once you're done with this mini boot camp, you'll be in shape to profit from your rewards card. And really, that's the only reason to use rewards cards.

First, however, we'll talk about cash back cards, which are wildly popular. And what's not to like? We all love some cold hard cash. Cash is king!

Cash back credit cards

This category of rewards cards covers a lot of different areas. You can get cash back cards where you earn cash back on everything. Or cash back on specific categories and at different rates.

How rewards are earned. You'll earn rewards as a percentage of what you've spent or as points per dollar.

Example: You get 1 percent cash back on all purchases.

This means you get 1 percent cash back for each dollar spent. If you spend \$100, you've earned 1 dollar ($100 \times .01 = \$1$).

Example: You get one point per dollar spent.

The fine print will give the point value. The baseline is that one point equals one cent. Again, if you spend $100, you earn one dollar.

Many credit card issuers have a trademarked name for the "currency" you earn. For example, American Express uses Reward Dollars, Discover uses Cashback Bonus, and Citi uses Dividend Dollars for its cash back card, the Citi Dividend Platinum Select Card.

Types of cash back cards

I'm going to give some specific examples here, but keep in mind that the terms change now and then. So you always need to read the current disclosure statements to make sure you have the most up-to-date information. Here are a few of the different rewards programs you'll see with cash back cards:

Cash back on everyday expenses with no specific categories. With this type of card, you don't have to think very much. You earn rewards on everything you purchase, but you don't get any bonuses in specific categories.

Example: The Capital One Quicksilver Cash Rewards Credit Card gives 1.5 percent on all purchases. You don't have to think about categories and some folks prefer that.

Cash back on everyday expenses with two or more special categories. You get cash back on all purchases, but a higher percent on specific categories.

Example: Blue Cash Everyday from American Express gives you 3 percent cash back on groceries (up to $6,000; then you get 1 percent), 2 percent on gas and select department stores, and 1 percent on everything else.

Sometimes, you'll see a "preferred" version of a rewards card. You get more rewards, but there's usually an annual fee. Here's the souped-up version of the Blue Cash Everyday Card: the Blue Cash Preferred Card from American Express. You get 6 percent cash back on groceries (up to $6,000; then you get 1 percent), 3 percent on gas and select department stores, and 1 percent on everything else.

Cash back on everyday expenses with five percent bonus categories that rotate every quarter. These cards are really cool, but you do have to pay attention to take advantage of them. The categories are usually very popular, like gas and restaurants, and they change every three months. You have to enroll for the bonus categories online to be eligible.

Co-branded, store, or retail cards

Cash back cards linked to a brand or store can be categorized as co-branded, store, or retail cards. A co-branded card has the retailer's brand, the credit card company's name, and logo of a payment network, such as Visa or MasterCard.

Some credit cards are designed to help you finance a big purchase. Some of these cards in this category have high interest rates. The appeal is that they're often easier to get than other consumer cards and if you shop frequently in a certain store, you can earn rewards.

Example of a co-branded card. TrueEarnings Card from Costco and American Express is an instance of a co-branded card. You get rewards while shopping at Costco as well as anywhere that American Express is accepted. Co-branded cards offer more shopping flexibility.

Example of a store charge card. Kohl's charge card, which really isn't a charge card, is one such instance. Charge cards don't allow you to revolve a balance. But stores like to call their cards charge cards for some reason. The Kohl's card lists an APR and a grace period, but you can only use the card and earn rewards at Kohl's.

The Kohl's card is issued by Capital One, but because it isn't co-branded with Visa, MasterCard, American Express, or Discover, it can only be used at Kohl's. However, the reason folks get store cards is because they shop at a place often and want to earn rewards. The rates for these kinds of cards, though, are usually high.

Example of a consumer credit card used to finance a large purchase. The Home Depot Consumer Credit Card offers six months of free financing for purchases in excess of $299. You start getting charged interest after six months. This type of card helps you finance an expensive purchase. For some people, this is the only way they can afford a new fridge.

Store rewards cards. These cards aren't credit cards, but I want to mention them because it can get confusing. An example is the Kroger Plus Rewards card. I have this card and I get rewards that I can use to pay for gas when I purchase it at the Kroger gas station.

I also have a Sephora rewards card, which is called Beauty Insider. I do a lot of video and TV, so I spend a lot on makeup. This helps me buy products I need at a discount. Plus, I earn free makeup. Anyway, don't confuse a store rewards card with a store credit card.

Travel rewards credit cards

If you love to travel, you can save lots of money if you use travel rewards credit cards strategically. You can focus on one area, such as saving on airline tickets, or take a broad approach.

Like its cash back counterpart, travel rewards cards come in all shapes and sizes. There are general travel rewards cards that focus on travel, but also offer you other redemption options. And there are airline-branded and hotel-branded cards that reward you for your loyalty to one brand.

How rewards are earned. You'll earn rewards as miles or points per dollar spent.

Example: You get one mile per dollar spent on all purchases.

The baseline is that one mile equals one cent. This means that if you spend $100, you earn one mile. If you have a card that offers two miles per dollar spent, then you earn two miles when you spend one dollar.

Example: You get one point per dollar spent.

The fine print will give the point value and it can vary based on your redemption choice. The baseline is that one point equals one cent.

General travel rewards credit cards. These cards give you the flexibility to fly on different airlines. And you earn miles or points that you can redeem for travel or other options, such as a statement credit or a gift card.

Example: Capital One Venture Card is a rewards card where you earn double miles for each dollar spent. If you spend $1,000, you've earned 2,000 miles. One mile, in this case, equals .01. So, 2,000 miles is worth $20 toward airfare or other redemption options. This is the I-don't-want-to-think-hard travel rewards program. I like it!

Airline-branded and hotel-branded cards

Airline-branded cards are perfect for the consumer who flies just about exclusively on one airline. The rewards can be very good if you fly frequently. And you get nice perks, like priority boarding, if that interests you.

Example: The Gold Delta Skymiles Credit Card gives you double miles on Delta purchases and one mile per dollar spent on all else. Baggage fees are waived for the first bag and you get a discount on in-flight purchases. You also get perks, like priority boarding.

I'll make a confession. (What's one more, right?) In the story at the start of this chapter, I got a credit card with a 30,000-mile bonus. That card is the Gold Delta. I live in Atlanta and I fly this airline almost exclusively. I also like priority boarding. I'm kind of petite and I like to get on the plane and stake out my area without getting shoved around. This is a perfect example of what I mean when I say you have to pick a card that works with your lifestyle and with your preferences.

Hotel-branded cards are specifically co-branded with a hotel. Often, these cards have generous rewards and if you are loyal to a particular hotel group, you can earn free nights and all kinds of good stuff.

Example: Marriott Rewards Visa Signature Card offers three points per dollar spent at Marriott hotels. Remember: We already talked about "preferred" versions of rewards cards. Another word often used is "premier."

Here's the Marriott Rewards card's more generous version: Marriott Rewards Premier Visa Signature Card. You get five points per dollar spent at Marriot hotels and there are no foreign transaction fees, plus many more perks and freebies.

General points

General points cards are difficult to pin down. You earn rewards in points and you get a wide variety of choices for redemption options. Some cards can be placed in the travel rewards category, the cash back category, and in the points category.

Example: The Citi ThankYou Card offers one point per dollar spent and recently, two points per dollar spent on dining and entertainment. You can redeem your points for a wide variety of rewards, including a check in $50 or $100 denominations, electronics, gift cards, CDs and DVDs, jewelry, toys, sporting goods, travel, and tons more.

You can also use your points to get a wish fulfilled by contacting one of Citi's Wish Specialists. Seriously, you can go parasailing, build the biggest and baddest sandcastle on an exotic beach, or get opera lessons.

I think I'd wish for a week (or a month) on an exotic beach, but without the hassle of building a castle. I just need a fruity concoction with a tiny umbrella in it and a somewhat trashy mystery novel.

Charge Cards

With charge cards, you have to pay your entire balance in full every month. These aren't credit cards because you can't revolve a balance. If you do slip up and revolve, you get penalized.

American Express has some excellent and famous (the Gold Card) charge cards, and they have nice rewards. There's The Basic (blue) Card, The Green Card, The Gold Card, and The Platinum Card. The annual fees range from zero for The Basic Card up to $450 for The Platinum Card. The higher the annual fee, the better the rewards get. As you can imagine, the perks also get better as you climb the American Express charge card ladder.

American Express also has a set business charge cards. Chase offers a charge card, the Ink Bold Business Charge Card, and it's pretty good. There's also the oldie, but goodie, the Diner's Club Card.

Rewards: fine print boot camp

I thought about calling this a Fine Print Spa, but I didn't think you'd buy it. How about this? You make it through my Rewards Fine Print Boot Camp and then go reward yourself with a spa day. And use a rewards card so you get cash back or miles.

In Chapter 4, I explained the APRs and credit card fees that you find in—and under—the Schumer Box. Here, I'll go into details about the kind of fine print that's unique to rewards credit cards. Remember: You won't see everything I cover on every card. But I'm giving you an overview so you're prepared for whatever you see out there.

Where is the fine print?

I mentioned earlier that it's sometimes hard to find all the details for rewards cards. Although this isn't always the case, you never know if you've actually read everything. And there's some disclosure material that you'll get in the mail after you get approved.

American Express does a great job of laying out all the rewards and perks. They have many that they're proud of and they want you to know about them. But I still have to leave the home page for a card and go to the Website for their loyalty program—Membership Rewards—to get details for the different levels of rewards.

I review rewards cards every day, so here's how I make sure that I cover my bases:

- I look all over the home page for the card. I click on links related to rewards. I click on "Offer Details" links.
- I read the footnotes on the home page.
- I look below the Schumer Box for rewards details. I click on any links that are in this section. Sometimes, there's a Web address and it isn't live. There's no excuse for that, but, as Tony Soprano used to say, "What're ya gonna do?"
- Google the name of the rewards program. Google something like this: "Discover cash back rewards" or "Chase ultimate rewards" or "Citi rewards program."
- If it's a cash back card with rotating categories, review the calendar of categories for the year. Most of the issuers have them.

Okay, you made like Magellan and you've found all of the fine print. There's some fine print jargon that's specific to rewards credit cards. Let's hop right into this and I'll show you how to decipher it without having to do a stint in law school.

Sign-up bonuses

Both cash back and travel rewards cards make good use of this marketing device. Note, however, that these offers are for new cardholders. Often, you'll see a statement like this: "This one-time bonus offer is valid only for first-time cardholders. Previous and current cardholders aren't eligible."

So if you've had the card in the past, you can't swoop in again and get the bonus. No double dipping. I've also seen language that says you aren't eligible if you have another card by the same issuer.

Also, it's usually stated that balance transfers and cash advances don't get applied to the bonus. They really want you to use the card to buy things. This gets them revenue from interchange fees, which I'll talk about more in the last chapter.

Usually, you spend a certain amount of money within a certain amount of time to get a certain amount of cash, miles, or points. Here's a cross-section of the kind of offers you'll see:

"One-time bonus of $100 once you spend $500 on eligible purchases within the first three months."

"If you spend $1,000 within the first three months, you earn 50,000 bonus points." This is for a hotel card and the points are enough for several free nights, depending on which category of hotel you choose.

"You earn a 10,000 mile bonus if you spend $1,000 within the first three months." This is worth $100 toward travel.

"Spend $500 within the first three months and earn 30,000 bonus miles." This is enough for a $300 ticket (plus taxes).

"Earn 5,000 bonus points, worth a $50 statement credit, after your first purchase."

Every credit card that offers a bonus will have its own set of requirements, and this is almost always highlighted on the home page. This is a huge marketing tool for issuers, so it's usually front and center (although you might have to look for details, such as what's eligible). Often, the issuer will have an "offer details" link on the home page.

Annual fees for rewards credit cards

There are several really good cash back cards that don't have annual fees, but most rewards credit cards do. The annual fee helps the credit card issuers pay for the rewards they're paying to consumers. Remember they're for-profit companies so rewards are offset by fees. But if you play the game right, you'll come out way ahead.

Most consumers don't take advantage of their rewards. So credit card companies know they can still profit from rewards cards because cardholders are paying annual fees and then not using the card in a way to maximize rewards. And people often never redeem the rewards they earn. I'll tell you how to avoid that fate when we talk about tracking rewards later in this chapter.

Annual fees range from zero to several hundred dollars. Do you remember the Platinum Card from American Express that I talked about earlier that comes with a $450 annual fee? There are super-elite credit cards for high net worth individuals that have annual fees much higher than that. Getting accurate information on the cards is difficult because card membership is by invitation only. You have to be really rolling in the dough and a very big spender to get invited to apply. One such card is American Express's The Centurion Card, also known simply as the Black Card. It's said that the initiation fee is $5,000 and that doesn't include the $2,500 annual fee. (Oddly enough, I haven't received my invitation for The Centurion Card yet. I'll share the details with you the moment I get my invite!)

Okay, back to reality and the rewards cards for the rest of us. Waiving the annual fee for the first year is a trend that has gone on for a few years. This is a nice perk and it gives you a year to build up rewards, so you offset the cost of the annual fee when it kicks in the next year.

When there's an annual fee involved, it's important to check your scorecard now and then. Are your rewards earnings out-weighing the cost of the annual fee? If not, are you so enamored of with the perks that you can afford to pay the fee without blinking? Some folks don't believe in ever paying an annual fee. That's perfectly fine. You have to go with what you're comfortable with.

Caps on category earnings

This often happens with category rewards. For instance, the Blue Cash Everyday Card lets you earn 3 percent on groceries, but this is capped at $6,000. The steroid version, Blue Cash Preferred, gives you a whopping 6 percent on groceries, but has the same cap.

Would you believe this grocery reward used to be unlimited? Cardholders used this card to buy loads of gift cards, such as Home Depot and Amazon at the grocery store. This is what's called "rewards hacking" and it isn't unusual, although it's more common with travel rewards. Americans are creative and savvy. Give them 6 percent cash back at the grocery store, and by golly, they'll figure out how to save at Home Depot. This is what happens when a good thing is taken to extremes. It started costing American Express too much, so they had to throw in a $6,000 cap.

Does it sound like I'm scolding rewards hackers? Actually, I'm not. I'm just telling you why the cap happened. I don't personally think that taking it to extremes is "unfair," although I don't do it myself often. I'm a rewards junkie, which means I take advantage of my rewards cards. But I'm not a hacker who spends time figuring out how to use the card in ways it wasn't intended.

The reason I don't do it is because I don't want to spend that much time on it. I run a business and I work a lot of hours. I also have two kids and an emotionally needy Maltese. Seriously, if there was a support group for puppies who love too much, I'd send him.

So I don't want to add anything to my to-do list. I don't want to think about all the extra gift cards I bought with my credit card or where I put all those gift cards. But then, I have a hard time remembering to use coupons even when I'm holding the coupon in my hand at the checkout. But for those who are willing to put in the time, I salute you! I will cover all kinds of rewards hacking in Chapter 11 so, if this appeals to you, you'll like that chapter a lot.

Rotating categories

While we're talking about caps, it's a good time to tell you what you need to know about cash back cards that have rotating categories. There's usually a link on the home page that takes you to the calendar where you can see the categories for each quarter.

Let's use the Chase Freedom Visa card as an example. Here are some typical categories you'll see during the year: gas stations, restaurants, theme parks, drug stores, and movie theaters. A new trend is to partner with a retail store. During 2013, Starbucks, Lowe's, Amazon.com, and Kohl's all partnered with Chase.

The 5 percent bonus category for fall 2013 (that's October through December) is Amazon.com and select department stores. Notice how timely this is for the holidays. Right now, Chase has a $1,500 cap set for the 5 percent bonus categories. After that, you get one percent.

So let's say you spend $1,500 at department stores during the holiday season. You'd get $75 cash back on this deal. After you hit the cap, you still get 1 percent, and there's not usually a limit on that. If you spend to the cap every quarter, you get an extra $300 per year. You don't get rich from it, but it's money you didn't have before. This is assuming, of course, that you use the card for purchases you needed to buy anyway. Otherwise, you're throwing money away to get rewards and that doesn't make any sense at all.

It is important to note that you do not get the 5 percent category bonus unless you register online. It's easy to do, so just set up a reminder on your calendar to do this each quarter. If you go to the dashboard where you sign up, there are usually options for setting up reminders.

Rewards by type of category

We talked about the 5 percent bonus categories, but this is different. Some cash back cards have category rewards that last all year as opposed to capped 5 percent bonus rewards that change quarterly.

Do you remember the Blue Cash Preferred Card that offers 6 percent grocery rewards (up to $6,000)? This card also offers an unlimited 3 percent at gas stations and department stores, and 1 percent on everything else.

These categories don't change unless you get a notice from your card issuer, which, in this case, is American Express. The fine print tells you if there's a cap (note the $6,000 on groceries) or if the rewards are unlimited.

Rewards based on tiers. With this system, you earn a certain percent or points up to a specified amount of purchases. For instance, you might get 3 percent on the first $20,000 spent and 2 percent on the next $20,000 spent. With a tiered system, the reward value per dollar spent is based on how much you spend over the course of the year.

Annual bonuses. Some credit cards offer an annual or an "anniversary" bonus as an added perk. These bonuses are offered in a variety of ways, and some come with requirements you must meet.

With hotel cards, it might be a free night's stay on your account anniversary. The Chase Sapphire Preferred offers a 7 percent anniversary bonus based on your total points earned in the year. So if you earned 50,000 points, you'd get a 3,500-point bonus. Some travel cards offer a companion ticket as an annual bonus.

In the fine print, you'll also find out if the bonus is based on the calendar year or on your account anniversary. Make sure you know the details so you don't miss out on any bonus you're owed.

Loss of rewards. Wouldn't it be awful if you carefully tracked your rewards and then lost them because you were late on a payment? In the fine print, you should find a list of actions that can trigger a loss of rewards.

Where is it? It could be anywhere, frankly. Most often, I see these clauses in the rewards information under the Schumer Box or in the rewards program details. Triggers include late payments, being in default on your account, or account inactivity. For inactivity, this will be defined by the individual card. And I've seen different inactivity requirements on two credit cards that have the same issuer.

Typically, you'll see that you can lose your rewards if your account is inactive for a period of time, usually 12 to 18 months, but

I've also seen six months as the cut-off. Some issuers might offer a chance to have your rewards reinstated for a fee. Or you might not have that opportunity at all, so be on your toes and don't do anything stupid to lose your rewards.

Special designations that come with exclusive rewards

Look on the front of your credit card. Do you see either "Visa Signature" or "World MasterCard" there? If so, you are entitled to an additional set of benefits, perks, and discounts.

Most issuers don't get into much detail about this. You'd think they'd want to stress the additional goodies. It's more difficult to get approved for cards with this designation, so maybe that's why they don't highlight it. Another reason could be that issuers have the freedom to decide if certain benefits won't be applied to one of their cards.

If you don't qualify for their card with a Visa Signature or World MasterCard designation, if they are a regular Visa or MasterCard version of the card, you might get approved for the lesser version.

Whatever the reason, the perks are very nice and here's a brief rundown of the benefits and where you can get more details. Do check with your card issuer to see if all of the Visa Signature or World MasterCard benefits apply to your card.

Visa Signature. Perks and benefits range from travel to shopping to sports. Throw in food and wine and entertainment, and there's a lot to be happy about. Here are some examples: no preset spending limits, travel-related benefits at luxury hotels including room upgrades, $25 food or beverage vouchers, late checkout, VIP guest status, and shopping discounts. Here's the home page where you can get more details about the perks and benefits: *https://usa.visa.com/visasignature/index.jsp*.

World MasterCard. Perks and benefits target frequent travelers, but there are also plenty of goodies for homebodies, too. Here are some examples: no pre-set spending limit, extended manufacturer's warranties, hotel room upgrades, preferred access to restaurant reservations, premium Broadway seats, a concierge service, price protection, and access to the Premium Collection. The Premium Collection is described as "offers for enhanced living." (That sounds good to me.)

If your trip gets canceled, either by you or the airline, you can get a refund of up to $1,500. Note, though, that if you cancel, it has to be on the "covered reason" list.

Here's the home page where you can get more details about the perks and benefits: *www.mastercard.us/credit-card-world.html*. And here's an additional Website with detailed information: *www. mastercard.com/us/personal/en/about ourcards/credit/world_card_ benefits.html#false.*

There's also a World Elite MasterCard, which is a step up from the World MasterCard designation. You get perks and service, such as an on-call travel advisor who will help you plan unique travel experiences or insider opportunities to exclusive events. Basically, you get help to do really expensive things.

Smart chip technology

When a credit card has a smart chip, it means the card is embedded with a microchip that encrypts cardholder information into a unique code. Most credit cards in the United States are magnetic stripe cards. On the back of the card, there's a magnetic stripe that contains your account information. When the card is swiped, the information is "read" by whatever device is being used to take your payment. The magstripe cards can be easily cloned, making them a fraud risk.

Credit cards with smart chips are more secure because the unique code is hard to duplicate. When you travel overseas, you might run into a problem if you're trying to use a magstripe card at a location that doesn't have the ability to process a swipe card.

With the smart chip card, you wave it across a chip-enabled terminal. In Chapter 12, I get into much more detail about why credit card technologies are hot and what it means for the future. But for now, all you need to know is that if your card has a smart chip, it's more secure and it's more likely to be accepted overseas.

Access to airport lounges

If you sometimes feel like you live in airports, then the benefits of being able to plop yourself down in a nice airport lounge is a perk you can appreciate. Like most rewards, this benefit varies a lot by card. If the benefit given is generous, the issuer will really tout this on the home page because it knows it's coveted by frequent travelers.

Priority Pass is an independent airport lounge network, which includes over 600 airport lounges. If you have a credit card that participates, like the American Express Platinum card, you get access to the lounges as long as you have a Priority Pass card and a ticket.

Or, if it's an airline-branded card, then you might get access to that airline's lounge. Other perks might include bringing a guest or extending privileges to your immediate family. For example, the Citi Executive/AAdvantage World Elite MasterCard gives you and your family access to the Admirals Club, American Airline's lounge.

Reward tiers and status levels

This is one of the most brilliant marketing techniques ever. People love participating in things where they can achieve a higher level. I think it's the sense of accomplishment you feel. Another incentive is the joy of being treated in a special way when you reach an elite status. Travel rewards card issuers know consumers love to feel special.

Let's look at an example: Hilton HHonors rewards program. Hilton hotels have four membership tiers: blue, silver, gold, and diamond. The basic level is blue and you get that just by enrolling in the program. To achieve the next tier, the Website says you need to stay at Hilton hotels more or achieve elite status faster by getting a Hilton HHonors *credit card*, which is conveniently linked to the card's home page.

There are actually two different Hilton cards: one from Citi and one from American Express. I'm going to use the Citi Hilton HHonors Reserve Card for this example.

With the Citi card, you get bumped up to gold status just by having the card. You jumped over silver! With gold elite status, you are treated quite well. You receive a 25 percent bonus on all the points you earn, opportunities for free nights, complimentary Wi-Fi, and lots more.

With your credit card, you'll earn points even on purchases away from Hilton. So if you travel a lot and stay at a Hilton property, you get points for paying for your stay, points for travel, and points for anything else you buy.

Airlines also have their own status levels. For instance, Delta has four elite status tiers:

- Silver: 25,000 MDM (Medallion Qualification Miles).
- Gold: 50,000 MDM (Medallion Qualification Miles).
- Platinum: 75,000 MDM (Medallion Qualification Miles).
- Diamond: 125,000 MDM (Medallion Qualification Miles).

When you get a Delta-branded credit card, you earn more miles when you make Delta purchases, but you also earn miles on all other purchases. If these programs are important to you, then take the time to understand how they work so you can climb the ladder and get the perks you deserve.

Transferring points to partner programs

A lot of frequent flyer programs allow you to transfer miles or convert points from their program to another program. And some credit cards let you convert points into miles. This, of course, is specific to each credit card and I'd have to write an entire book to explain every possibility.

So if this is important to you, this is one of those areas you need to check out before you get a travels card. With the Chase Sapphire Preferred card, for instance, you can transfer points you've earned to your choice of partner programs. This includes airlines, hotels, and Amtrak.

These programs can get confusing, especially when you're converting points into miles. Don't hesitate to call customer service and ask for clarification if you need to.

Companion certificates

Want to hear something weird? While I was writing this chapter last summer, my companion certificate for my Gold Delta Card from American Express popped into my inbox. I've been expecting it and it was super cool to actually see it.

This is another one of those "anniversary" bonuses. As I read the e-mail, though, I was disappointed that it also said this was the last one I'd receive because they were no longer awarding the bonus to Gold Card members.

This is why you need to read all correspondence you get from your card issuer. Card companies can change your rewards at any time. However, I do give Delta and American Express marks for making good on this reward. They could have just changed it and said tough luck to all of us.

If you do have a card that offers a companion ticket, please note the expiration date. I have one year to use my certificate and there's not a snowball's chance in hell that I will let this baby expire.

Tracking rewards

Have you wasted any of your rewards in the past? You can be honest, if you have. I've done it and I'm supposed to know what I'm doing. Recent research has shown that many people waste rewards. This doesn't surprise me because it takes effort to keep track of points, miles, and cash back on several cards.

According to a 2011 study by COLLOQUY (available at *www. colloquy.com*), Americans accumulate around $48 billion worth of miles and points every year. Think about what a huge amount that is. A third of the rewards—roughly $16 billion—go unredeemed. Now, let's look at a sample size we can wrap our heads around. The average consumer earns $622 per year in rewards and leaves $205 of that on the table.

Wasting rewards, however, isn't the only problem. People also don't understand how they work. A national survey done by ThePointsGuy.com and the Princeton Group showed that 73 percent of Americans who have frequent flyer miles "don't know how many they have and 59 percent said they don't know how these programs work."

So there are two things to keep in mind. First, understand how your rewards program works. Second, track the darn rewards and use them. Here are two Websites that I like a lot for tracking rewards. They also have mobile options so you can keep track while on the go.

AwardWallet.com. According to this Website, "There are an estimated 10 trillion unused frequent-flier miles in circulation worth over $165 billion." Well, that's a lot of miles. This Website has been around since 2004 and supports 562 loyalty programs, including air, credit cards, hotel, car rental, and others. A basic membership is free, but you have the option to pay for an upgrade and get snazzier tools.

Website: *https://awardwallet.com/*.
Phone Apps: Android, iPhone.

Tripit's Point Tracker. Point Tracker is part of TripIt Pro and it tracks more than 120 programs. It monitors expiration dates, shows you what miles you need to reach the next level, and more.

Website: *www.tripit.com/pointtracker.*

TripIt Mobile: Android, iPhone, iPad, Blackberry, Windows Phone 7.

Using travel rewards cards overseas

When you use a credit card overseas and you're asked if you want to be billed in the local foreign currency or in U.S. dollars, you should say the local currency. If you're billed in U.S. dollars, you usually don't get the best rate because the vendor gets a cut. This is called Dynamic Currency Conversion.

Even if you're using a credit card with no foreign transaction fees, this can cost you money. Another fly in the ointment is the exchange rate. According to a CardHub Currency Exchange Study, the exchange rates that banks can charge vary a lot. But the study results still showed that cardholders saved the most money when they used credit cards with no foreign transaction fees and avoided dynamic currency conversion.

8

The Good and the Bad
of Business Cards

During the recent recession, small businesses had a difficult time trying to get small business loans from banks. Credit was beyond tight. So it's not surprising that a 2010 report by the Federal Reserve showed that 83 percent of business owners used credit cards in the course of business. And 64 percent specifically used small business credit cards. Only 12 percent of small businesses borrow money using their credit cards.

Recently, however, there has been cause for optimism. According to an April 2013 FICO survey, U.S. bank risk managers said that "62 percent of respondents said the supply of credit for small business loans in the next six months would satisfy demand, and 89 percent said the approval rate for small business loans would hold steady or increase" (*www.fico.com/en/Company/News/Pages/4-16-2013-FICO-Survey-Finds-Credit-Spigot-Opening-for-Small-Businesses.aspx*).

What's good about business credit cards

Clearly, small business credit cards are an important part of running a business, even if it's just to track expenses. Once you get a business credit card, you can start taking steps to build credit in your business's name.

I'm sure there are entire books written about organizing your personal and business expenses, so I'm not going to get into the logistics of it. Personally, I like zip-lock bags for receipts. (Please don't tell anyone I'm too cheap to buy containers.) I'm just going to zero in on how this relates to credit cards because there's this corporate veil thing to worry about.

Do not pierce the corporate veil

Don't do it, because if you do, you could be sorry. First, let me absolve myself from any blame whatsoever. I'm giving you my opinion and also what I've learned from becoming an LLC myself. Laws are different in every state, so the advice I'm giving should be used as a guideline for behavior and not as a rule of law.

One of the biggest advantages of incorporating your business is to protect yourself from being held personally liable. If you're sued or have a liability for any reason, the opposing attorney will go after the company's assets. After that avenue is exhausted, though, he or she could try to get to your personal assets.

This is called piercing the corporate veil. Now, there are many factors that go into determining if the veil has been pierced. But one thing that is usually considered is if you used corporate resources for your personal life.

There are many ways, including cash and loans, where a person could stick their hand in the corporate coffers for personal use. But let's stick with credit cards here. If you have a credit card that you've designated as your business card, then you should never, ever put personal expenses on it.

In early 2013, I became Harzog Enterprises LLC. I did this for a variety of reasons. After my business became a legal entity, I chose a credit card to use strictly for my business expenses.

Just a few weeks later, I was at the drug store picking up a prescription for my allergies. After I got in line, I remembered that my daughter, who was home from college for the summer, had my debit card because I was paying for some things she needed. My son had my Discover card to pay for books he needed for a summer assignment. I have several credit cards and I usually have them with me, but I'd changed purses in a hurry that morning. I'm sure you ladies can relate to this.

The only card in my wallet was my business credit card. I thought about it. I thought about the time it would take to drive back home and get a different credit card. It would've been so easy to stay there and use my business card.

Then I thought about the corporate veil. I wasn't going to risk it. I drove home and got another card and drove back to the drug store. Pick your business credit card and don't use it for anything else, even when you find yourself in a situation where using it is very convenient. Just say no to combining personal and business expenses.

I want you to take your time and pick a business card that works for your business. It really is an important decision. Sure, you can always change cards, but it's nice to stick with one card that meets your needs so you don't have to combine financial information when you do your taxes.

Management tools

One of the main advantages of using a business credit card is that you often get great management tools. Here's a snippet of features that are available on many business credit cards:

- Detailed statements that can categorize your purchases.
- Alerts when employees make a purchase.

- ◆ Caps on employee spending as a whole or by employee.
- ◆ Tax reports.
- ◆ Year-end summaries.
- ◆ Ability to download your purchase records into different formats, such as Quicken, Excel, and QuickBooks.

And more cards than ever have mobile apps so you can keep tabs on your business when you're on the go.

The dark side of business credit cards

Business credit cards have a split personality. They've got kind of a Dr. Jekyll and Mr. Hyde thing going on. There's a delightful Dr. Jekyll side that offers excellent management tools and reward programs.

However, the Mr. Hyde side lurks underneath. Business credit cards are not covered by the Credit CARD Act of 2009. So you don't have all the protections you get with consumer credit cards. There are exceptions, but these are based on individual decisions by each bank. I'll point these out later in this chapter.

About every six to nine months, the media will come out with this as if it's breaking news. It's been old news since February 21, 2010, when the first part of the CARD Act took effect.

I can only speculate here, but I'm guessing that to get this legislation passed, a lot of compromises had to be made. Somewhere along the way, it was decided that credit cards for small business would not be covered by the CARD Act. I think the public and the media have a short-term memory about this because it's businesses that are getting screwed, not consumers. So once or twice a year we get an outraged "Can you believe this?" headline.

CARD Act protections you don't get

I want you to be clear about the protections you don't get with business credit cards. Let's do a quick overview and then we'll get to your business and credit history. You learned about the Credit CARD Act of 2009 in Chapter 2. Read that section again to make sure you know the difference in protections between consumer and business cards. Well, business credit cards don't get that protection. Take a look at what can happen when you use a business card.

I'm not going to go over the CARD Act again, but I do want to highlight a few of the more dangerous aspects because they need to be top of mind. But don't freak out, I'll give you some tips next to help you protect yourself.

No protection against sudden interest rate increases. With consumer cards, you get protection against APR increases for the first year (with a few exceptions). But even if you get an APR increase later on, you get 45 days notice that your rate has been increased.

With business cards, there are no protections against APR increases. The issuer can hike your rate from 12 percent to 18 percent overnight. The best issuers will send you a notice, but don't depend on much advance notice, if any.

APR increases can be applied to your outstanding balance. This one can get you into a mess of trouble. Let's say you're carrying a balance of $2,000 because you needed some new equipment for your business. But then APR goes up from 13 percent to 19 percent. Suddenly, you're paying 19 percent on your new purchases as well as on your outstanding balance.

Payments over the minimum may not go to highest APR balances first. Banks apply the amount in excess of your minimum payment any way they like. They may choose to apply the excess to your highest APR balance, but they aren't required to. You can find out how this situation is handled in the fine print.

Universal default. Before the CARD Act, your credit card issuer could increase your APR on your credit card if you showed an increase of risk with another lender. For example, if you missed a credit card payment with Bank A, Bank B could see that as a bad sign and increase your APR on the credit card you have with Bank B. It could even be unrelated to credit cards. You could be late on your car loan and trigger the "universal default" reaction.

With business cards, though, this can still happen. I've seen statements about this in the Schumer Box in the section where the penalty APR is. It suggests that you might get the default APR if you make a late payment, bounce a check, or exceed your credit limit on any accounts or loans that you have with the bank.

I've also seen vague phrases such as "other indications of account performance" when talking about what might trigger an increase. At least some issuers let you know it's a possibility. It's often not even mentioned, and this is perfectly legal too.

There's no requirement for credit card mailing dates. With consumer cards that offer grace periods, they have to mail the statement at least 21 days before your payment is due. But with business cards, there's no standard for the time they have to give you. You could have a situation where you get your statement and the bill is due in less than two weeks. So pay attention to the due date when you look at the statement.

Double-cycle billing isn't banned. This is a balance computation method. When this method is used, the issuer can apply interest charges to two full cycles of card balances instead of just the current one. Therefore, even if you paid off your entire credit card balance in one month, you could still be charged interest in the following month.

Credit card companies that apply the CARD Act anyway

I salute the banks that do this, even if only partially. But remember: They're doing this voluntarily. If the economy shifts and it's not in their best interests anymore, these policies could change. So don't relax and think you have no worries.

CardHub recently conducted the 2013 Small Business Credit Card Study, which you can find at CardHub.com, and reported on which credit card issuers apply at least parts of the CARD Act to business cards. CardHub does a lot of original research, and I often find their reports fascinating. The study showed that "Bank of America is the most small business friendly credit card issuer, as it's the only one to have extended all of the major CARD Act protections to its business-branded cards" (*www.cardhub.com/ edu/2013-small-business-credit-card-study/*).

The study also showed that all the major issuers apply at least some of the CARD Act protections to business cards. But again, keep in mind that these policies are voluntary. And no matter what you read on the Internet, always follow up with your bank to confirm what CARD Act protections it offers on its business credit cards.

Protect yourself

You're the boss of your credit card issuer, not the other way around. I said this in Chapter 1 and I meant it. Here's what you can do to protect yourself and stand your ground when necessary:

- Read everything from your issuer. I don't care if it's e-mail, snail mail, phone, or Morse code. You are not being proactive if you're surprised by APR increases or fees.

- You can choose to use a consumer card for your business expenses if your business is simple. Just be sure that card is dedicated to business expenses only. Remember the corporate veil.

- Pay off balances every month or keep balances as low as you can. If you need to carry debt for capital reasons or cash flow and it's not short-term, try a bank loan (low APR and better terms) or maybe social lending, like LendingClub or Prosper.

Again, you're the boss and don't ever forget it. When things don't go well, call and negotiate. Threaten to move to a different card. There's a belief that banks only want customers who carry a balance and that's not true. They also need people who are great customers or their business won't survive. If you've got excellent credit, you're valuable to every bank out there.

Shortly after the CARD Act took effect, I recall that there was an increase of business card mailings to consumers. At the time, it was speculated that issuers were trying to catch consumers off guard. It was some kind of ploy to get them to apply for business cards instead of consumer cards.

I'm not sure that it was an orchestrated effort, but I'd bet some consumers did slip up and apply for these particular cards. You don't have to be incorporated to get them. At the end of the day, though, it doesn't matter if there was evil afoot. It's your job to protect yourself and you can do that by staying informed.

Is your personal credit history important?

In a word, yes. I know we're talking about business cards, but unless you have a track record of success and profit, your personal credit history remains very important.

CardHub's Small Business Credit Card Study also asked issuers questions about how important personal credit history is when a consumer is applying for a business card. Here are some highlights from the study:

- All of the "major credit card companies holds its customers personally liable for business credit card use."
- Every major issuer (except for Barclaycard USA and USAA, because they don't offer business credit cards) reports delinquent payments to your personal credit reports.
- "Every major credit card issuer uses personal credit history to determine eligibility for a business credit card" (CardHub.com).

Unless your business has a financially successful track record, the credit card company will use your personal credit history to make a decision about your business credit card application. If you don't have a good personal credit history, it will be difficult for you to get a business credit card. So basically, in order to build business credit, you need to start by making sure you have excellent personal credit.

If you skipped Chapter 2, I won't scold you, but I will ask you to go take a look at it now. You need to understand how to check your personal credit reports and score before you can get going on your business credit. Does this mean that your payment history with your business credit card will show up on your personal credit history? Probably not, but this can vary according to issuer.

On the other hand, if you default or miss payments the negative information could show up on your personal credit history. So, you could have a situation where you don't get personal credit (and the associated boost in your FICO score) when things go well. But if anything negative happens, your personal credit report and score could suffer.

Building business credit is a complex topic, so I can't give you everything you need to know here. However, check out the Education Center on the Dun & Bradstreet Website (*www.dandb. com/credit-resources/business-credit/*) to get the steps to building business credit. You'll get advice for expanding the number of trade accounts on your report and developing a good credit score.

Different types of business credit cards

Just like consumer credit cards, there are different types of business cards. The types of cards are similar, but of course, the fine print is a little different.

General credit card with no rewards. You can get a business credit card without rewards, if you prefer. This is a good choice for the business owner who has low overhead and is just interested mainly in separating personal and business expenses.

Rewards credit cards. You can get a general overview of these cards in Chapter 7. Cash back cards are a good choice if saving on everyday expenses is important to you. A card that offers travel rewards is a good idea if you or your employees travel a lot. And, just like with consumer cards, you can get credit cards that focus on a particular need, like gas expenses, cellular service, or hotel expenses.

Business secured credit card. There are even secured credit cards designed for businesses that need to rebuild. Like with a consumer secured card, you have to make a deposit to secure the card. You don't see many of these. An example is the Wells Fargo Business Secured Credit Card.

How to find them

You can use the same techniques that you use to find and compare consumer credit cards. Check out the credit card comparison Websites and you'll see a business credit card category. Google "business credit cards" and read consumer reviews in forums. I review business credit cards on my Website, so, if you can't find a review for a card that you're interested in, send me a request for a review.

Take your time to make sure you get a card that fits your needs. Think about what your biggest expenses are so you can drill down on a specific category. Or you might decide that your needs are more generic and you'd prefer a points card that allows you to choose what types of rewards you need at any given time. The right card is the one that works for you.

The fine print of business credit cards reward programs

There's a lot of crossover when it comes to the details of the rewards programs. So I'm not going to reinvent the wheel. You'll be pleased to know there's no Rewards Fine Print Boot Camp!

If you're only interested in business cards and you skipped Chapter 4 about the fine print and Chapter 7 about rewards programs, you need to read those now. If you're in business, the chances are that you also have a consumer credit card, so this should be time well spent. Let's look at the categories we covered in Chapter 7 and I'll tell you what to expect that's different when you're researching business cards.

Types of cash back rewards

Just like with consumer cards, there's a variety of cash back business cards. Like I did in Chapter 7, I'm going to give specific examples because that's a good way for you to see what's out there. But again, remember that these are only examples and the terms change frequently. So always read the latest information on the card's home page. Here are a few of the different cash rewards program you'll see with business credit cards.

Cash back on everyday expenses with no specific categories. With this type of card, you don't have to think very much. You earn rewards on everything you purchase, but you don't get any bonuses in specific categories.

Example: The Capital One Spark Cash Select for Business gives 1 percent on all purchases, but then you also get a 50 percent annual bonus on the cash back you earn every year.

Cash back on everyday expenses with two or more special categories. You get cash back on all purchases, but a higher percent on specific categories. As you can imagine, the categories differ from consumer categories.

Example: SimplyCash Business Card from American Express gives you 5 percent cash back at U.S. office supply stores and on wireless phone service purchases directly from U.S. providers. You get 3 percent at U.S. gas stations, and 1 percent on everything else. (The 5 and 3 percent rebates are capped at $12,000 and then you get 1 percent.)

Cash back on rotating categories. This isn't very common among business cards, but I have a feeling we might be seeing more of this in the future. You can plan your expenses around the quarterly categories to maximize your profit.

Example: The CitiBusiness ThankYou Card offers three points per dollar spent on quarterly rotating categories. You get one ThankYou point per dollar spent on everything else.

Travel rewards credit cards

Some business credit cards offer some really good travel rewards. For the business owner who travels (or has employees who travel), these cards can save you a lot of money. You can get general travel rewards cards or go for an airline-branded card if you usually stick with one airline.

General travel rewards credit cards. Some people don't like to be stuck with one airline. Maybe you want to go with the best rate or the most convenient. If that's the case, a general travel rewards card is your best bet.

Example: Capital One Spark Miles for Business is a miles card where you earn double miles for each dollar spent. If you spend $2000, you've earned 4,000 miles. One mile, in this case, equals .01. So, 4,000 miles is worth $40 (4,000 × .01) toward airfare or other redemption options.

Airline-branded cards. These cards are perfect for the small business owner who flies just about exclusively on one airline. The rewards are usually excellent.

Example: The Gold Delta SkyMiles Business Credit Card from American Express gives you two miles per dollar spent on Delta purchases and one mile per dollar spent on all else. Baggage fees are waived for the first bag and you get a discount on in-flight purchases.

Hotel-branded cards. These business cards are co-branded with a hotel. You can use the card when you stay at one of the properties.

They often have flexible rewards and you can use your rewards airline travel as well as other options.

Example: Starwood Preferred Guest Business Credit Card from America Express gives you up to five Starpoints (I just love the name!) per dollar spent at Starwood properties, which includes the Westin and Sheraton hotels.

Gas-station branded cards. There are business versions of gas cards. Examples include the Chevron and Texaco Universal Business Card or the BP Business Solutions Fuel Program. Honestly, the high APRs don't impress me. I want you to know they're out there, but I also want you to know there are *so* many credit cards with better gas rewards and better terms.

I do know some business owners who got gas cards for the sheer purpose of building business credit. These cards are easier to get in your business's name than those from a major bank. But be careful if you go that route. (Yes, pun intended.)

General points credit cards. These are the credit cards that want to be everything you need. Some of them are really loaded with benefits and rewards.

Example: The Chase Ink Plus Business Card is a premium travel rewards credit card. You earn five points per dollar spent on the first $50,000 spent annually at office supply stores, and on cellular phone, land line, Internet, and cable TV services. This is just a sample of the rewards. It's an excellent business rewards card.

Business charge cards. If you've read Chapter 4, you know that with a charge card you have to pay your entire balance in full every month. If you don't have cash flow issues, you might consider this because they often have outstanding rewards. But they have annual fees, too.

American Express business charge cards are well-known and quite popular. It's kind of prestigious to have a business "Gold Card" from American Express. It's beyond prestigious to have the Business Platinum Card (but also expensive; it comes with a $450 annual fee).

Business credit cards: where is the fine print?

Just like with consumer cards, the fine print can be elusive, and sometimes you don't see everything until you get approved and you get a packet in the mail. You can stick with the previous suggestions that I covered in Chapters 4 and 7. Look for the fine print in these places: the home page for the card, any link with "Offer Details" on it, footnotes on the home page, the Schumer Box, and below the Schumer Box for rewards details. Also, just to be thorough, Google the name of the rewards program. For now, though, let's look at some fine print that's a little unique to business credit cards.

Sign-up bonuses. One big difference you'll see is the threshold for earning the bonus. Instead of $500, it might be $5,000. Most often, you'll still see the three-month requirement to earn the bonus. You'll still see some low spending requirements, but the better the card, the higher the spending requirement.

Annual fees. This works the same way as consumer cards do: the better the rewards, the higher the annual fee. But you can get some decent cash back credit cards without an annual fee. You'll also see annual fees waived for the year to make it attractive to you.

Caps on category earnings. Business cards that offer category rewards often have caps. For instance, the Chase Ink Cash Credit Card lets you earn 5 percent cash back on the first $25,000 spent annually at office supply stores, cellular phone, land line, Internet, and cable TV services. After you reach the cap, you earn 1 percent.

Rotating categories. There are several popular consumer cash back cards that have rotating categories. As I mentioned before, there aren't many business cards with this feature. The CitiBusiness ThankYou Card is an example, though. It offers three ThankYou points for every dollar spent in rotating categories, such as office supply merchants, advertising services, airlines, and entertainment. Unlike the consumer counterpart, though, the number of points you can earn with this card is unlimited.

Annual bonuses. Some credit cards offer an annual or an "anniversary" bonus as an added perk. With hotel cards, it might be a free night's stay on your account anniversary. The Marriott Rewards Business Credit Card offers 10 nights Elite status credit on your account anniversary date.

Again, be sure you know if the bonus is based on your account anniversary or on the calendar year. You'll often find an anniversary bonus with the better business credit cards. Sometimes the bonus will escalate. You might get a 1 percent bonus on the rewards you earned in your first year of card ownership. But in the second year, you might get 2 percent and then 3 percent thereafter.

Are you getting the idea that I don't trust card companies to give me what I've earned? "Trust, but verify," is my approach to just about everything now that I think about it.

Rewards based on tiers. This can be set up a variety of ways. Perhaps you get a certain number of points per dollar for the first $25,000 you spend, but then you get a lower number of points per dollar for the next $25,000.

With the CitiBusiness/AAdvantage World MasterCard, cardholders can earn a $99 domestic economy fare American Airlines Companion Certificate if they spend $30,000 or more in eligible purchases during the card membership year. This means each 12-month period prior to the account anniversary date.

There are often other requirements, too. In the case of the CitiBusiness/AAdvantage World MasterCard, the account has to remain open for a minimum of 45 days after your account anniversary date. So no grabbing the goodies and heading right out the door.

Access to airport lounges. This is a big perk with business owners who travel. Think about it. You can handle a little discomfort if you're flying off to Belize for a weekend of diving. But think about flying across the country in coach to meet a client. And then once you get there, you're sitting in a conference room all day.

Businesspeople who fly really benefit from lounge access. Comfort is important because business travel can be a bore. Note, however, even if the bullet points says "lounge access," that doesn't mean you get a free pass to every lounge. Some cards might offer two free passes to the airport lounge of your choice, but then you pay a discounted rate ($27 pops up often) for each visit after that.

Now, some elite cards (with big annual fees) might give you a free pass to lounges. There are a couple of big programs, Priority Pass and Lounge Club, so be aware of which program is used by your card. Read the details carefully so you know what you're actually getting—and *not* getting.

Employee cards. If you have employees, this is huge. Sometimes this information is on the home page. But sometimes you find it in the Schumer Box where the annual fee is listed. If there's an annual fee for each employee card, you'll find it there. Or it could be below the box. If you can't find the details, call the issuer and ask. There could also be a limit on the number of employee cards that are free, so it's important to get this question answered.

Additional card spending limits. If you have additional cards, this doesn't mean that the spending limit you receive will apply to the additional cards. You'll find out after you're approved, but I want you to know about this so your expectations are in line with reality.

Special incentives to pay your bill early. This isn't common, but I wouldn't be surprised to see this more often in the charge card arena. The Plum Card from American Express uses this feature. You get a discount for paying early, which I like.

Foreign transaction fees. I'm bringing this up because if you or your employees travel overseas frequently, it's important to get a card that waives these fees. The average fee is 3 percent and it adds up quicker than you think it will.

9

Get Out of Debt With a Balance Transfer Card

I f you're in credit card debt, you probably feel like you've got the weight of the world on your shoulders. Am I right? Of course I am. I know because I've been there and I felt like I was carrying a boulder.

One of the best ways to get rid of—or at least pay down—your credit card debt is to transfer your credit card to a balance transfer credit card that has a zero percent introductory APR.

Check your FICO score at the door

Everyone loves to tell you that a balance transfer is the best way to get out of debt. But often they don't tell you there's a catch. And it's not an itty-bitty catch, either. You must have excellent credit to get the best deals. This doesn't mean you can't still find a balance transfer card if your FICO score is less than 720.

If your debt is on a card (or cards) with a 22.99 percent APR, then transferring your debt to a card with a 12.99 percent APR still saves you interest expense. You probably can't get rid of your debt quickly that way, but sometimes baby steps will get you there. Once your score gets higher—and paying down a balance will help in that regard—you might qualify for better deals.

What if you're closer to 650 than 700? In Chapter 2, you learned about FICO scores and how you can't fix a bad one overnight. But if you can take nine months or a year to work on it, here are a few things to try:

- Pay *all* of your bills on time. Every single one, not just your credit card bills. It would be a crying shame to get reported to a credit bureau because you haven't paid your cell phone bill.

- Lower your credit card utilization ratio (the amount of credit used compared to the amount of available credit) as much as you can. This will be hard to do if your balances are on cards with high APRs.

- Don't close any credit card accounts, especially cards you've had for a long time.

- Don't open new credit card accounts. It's true you only get dinged two to five points, but if you're trying to get to 700, every point might be important.

- Make sure there are no errors on your annual credit reports.

The outcomes of trying to improve your score are unpredictable. Do your best, though, and you might see some good results. Once your score is high enough, you could qualify for a balance transfer card with excellent terms.

How does a balance transfer work?

It's not a difficult process, but there are many moving parts and timing issues. Now, the details will most likely vary by credit card issuer. Let's use an example to give you a basic idea of what happens when you request a balance transfer.

Meet Jessica, who is a 20-something marketing director. She has a penchant for luxury travel and fine dining. She suddenly finds herself in credit card debt to the tune of $5,000. What's worse is that her APR is 17 percent. (Yikes, right?)

Her FICO score is 720, which is about the minimum she'll need for the best deals. And, just so you know how much variance there is among credit card issuers, some banks will find this score acceptable, but others might want a score of at least 750.

Back to Jessica: She's researched balance transfer cards and has decided to transfer her $5,000 balance from her Old Credit Card to her New Credit Card. After she's approved for her New Credit Card and makes the request for a balance transfer, her New Bank pays $5,000 to her Old Bank. This pays off Jessica's $5,000 balance on her Old Credit Card.

This isn't instantaneous, however; it can take a few weeks. So Jessica, being the savvy woman that she is, keeps making payments on her Old Credit Card so she doesn't get hit with a late payment fee. When Jessica's New Bank notifies her that the balance transfer is complete, she follows up with her Old Bank to confirm that the balance on the Old Credit Card is zero.

Now that the balance transfer process is complete, Jessica starts making payments on her $5,000 balance to the New Bank because the debt is now on her New Credit Card. Jessica's New Credit Card has an 18-month zero percent introductory APR. So Jessica has 18 months to pay down her balance without accruing any interest.

That, folks, is how it's supposed to work. And it probably sounds simple enough, right? At a high level it is. But there's that annoying fine print that we have to talk about. Plus, there are common mistakes that consumers make that totally screw up their chance to get out debt.

How much money does Jessica save? There are several credit card calculators on the Internet. For this example, I used the one on the Federal Reserve's Website. On her old credit card, if Jessica makes a minimum payment of $100 each month, it will take her 30 years to pay off her balance. During that time, she will have paid $10,467 in interest charges. But if she doubles the payment to $200 per month, she pays it off in three years and pays $1,217 in interest charges.

Now, with her New Credit Card and zero percent APR, she has to pay $5,300 ($5,000 + $300 fee) total, so she needs to pay $294.44 per month to pay her debt off in 18 months. Jessica sticks with her payment time table. In 18 months, she's debt free and lets out a big sigh of relief followed by a giant smile. Because that's what you do when you get out of debt. You feel relief and unabashed joy.

Find the right balance transfer credit card

Do you remember in Chapter 2 when we talked about the credit card comparison Websites? Those Websites are a good place to start. You can also do a Google search for "best balance transfer credit cards" and put together your own list of candidates.

If you have really good credit, you've also probably gotten oodles of balance transfer offers in the mail. Being pre-approved doesn't mean you're already approved for the card, but it does mean the issuer thinks you have a good shot. So take a good look at these offers and see if they look like a good fit.

Credit card convenience checks

Instead of offers, you may have received the convenience checks in the mail for credit cards that you already have. These can be a little tricky.

If you've been a good customer, you'll start getting these. I've received as many as five checks in one envelope. Usually, the checks are different colors and they vary in terms. One check might have a zero percent introductory offer for six months, but it might have a short time frame to take advantage of the offer.

What makes it more confusing is that some of these can be used as a balance transfer and some as a cash advance. You might have two checks with one set of rules and another check with another set of terms. Only do this if you know exactly what you're doing. This is not a situation I recommend for anyone not used to reading fine print. Be afraid. Be *very* afraid.

In Chapter 11, you're going to learn about what I like to call "extreme credit." Here, I go over some risky maneuvers and I'll cover how you can use these balance transfer checks in ways they weren't intended.

The fine print for balance transfer credit cards

Don't look now, but this is our last set of fine print we're going to tackle. If you were thinking about heading for the hills to avoid another fine print explanation, relax. This is short and sweet.

In the Schumer Box, some of the balance transfer information is located just below the purchase APR. Notice I said that some of it is, not all of it. That would be too easy, wouldn't it?

This is one thing I'd like to change about the Schumer Box. The interest rates are separated from the fees for balance transfers and for cash advances. Often, the rest of the details or instructions are in the fine print below the box. So, most of the time, you have to look in three different spots.

APR for balance transfers. Here's where the introductory offer will be.

Length of the introductory offer. You'll see the length of the offer, for example, and it might be a zero percent introductory APR for 18 months. You want to figure out how long you need to pay it off.

In the example with Jessica, she needed 18 months to pay off her debt. But there are 12-month offers and 15-month offers, too. Unless there's an incentive to pay it off earlier, such as a waived transfer fee, I'd go with the longest offer. You never know what might happen that could cause you to need more time. But if you can pay it off in 15 months and the transfer is waived, go for it.

You'll save money on the fee and experience the lightness of being debt-free three months earlier.

The introductory offer deadline. Sometimes, this is listed with the length of the offer, but sometimes the deadline is in the fine print below the box. Wherever it is, you have to find it. If you can't find it, call the issuer and ask. Or ask via the chat feature that most of the major issuers have on the credit card's Website. A little box will pop up on your screen and ask if you have a question. I use this feature all the time, and it is quick and helpful.

You need to know the answer because I've seen offers that expired within 30 days. Usually, though, it's several months. In this spot, you'll also see the go-to rate. It might be one APR or it could be a range, such as 11.99 percent to 22.99 percent. You'll find out what your APR is when you get approved for the card, if it's a range.

This is the rate you'll have after the introductory period ends. If you still have a balance when the introductory period ends, then your balance will start accruing interest expense at this rate. The ongoing APR for purchases is almost always a variable rate these days. So your APR will vary based on the movement of the prime rate, which hasn't changed in quite a while.

Balance transfer fees. This is what I find annoying. Not the fee, but the location of the information. Okay, the fee is annoying, too. You have to look in the bottom section of the Schumer Box to find the transaction fee.

Under "Transaction Fees," the balance transfer fee is usually listed first. Typically, you'll see something like this: "Either $5 or three percent of the amount of each transfer, whichever is greater."

For the fee to be $5, you'd have to be transferring only $166.50 (166.50 × .03 = $4.995). The banks have themselves covered here because not many people will go to the trouble of a balance transfer for $166.50.

As my teen would say, "Whatever!" I don't know if the point is to trick you into thinking the fee could be that low. Usually, the fee is 3 percent, but I've seen 4 and 5 percent. As I mentioned in Chapter 4, once in a while you'll see a balance transfer fee waived altogether.

Balance transfer instructions. This is below the Schumer Box. It's vital that you read this section. The details will vary by card, but here's a sample of what you'll learn:

- The expiration date of the introductory offer.
- How long it takes to process the transfer.
- Instructions for canceling your balance transfer (before it's complete, of course).
- Restrictions on how you can use a balance transfer. For instance, an issuer might say you can't use a transfer to pay off another card with the same issuer. For example, you can't transfer a balance from the Escape by Discover card to the Discover it card.
- Information about how a balance transfer from more than one credit card will be handled.

Often, you'll see this line when the issuer is discussing balance transfers or the rewards program: "See your Card member Agreement for details." This line protects them legally. If you don't understand why you lost an introductory rate, well, it's all in the card member agreement. That's why you have to be the one to protect yourself. I point out as much as I can possibly find. But I am, after all, only one woman. So do your part and know what's in the fine print as best you can.

Loss of introductory APR. You'll see what you have to do to lose your rate. Often, I'll see "We will end your introductory APR if any required Minimum Payment is 60 days late, and apply the Penalty APR."

However, I've also seen this one: "We may end your introductory APR and apply the Penalty APR if you make a late payment." That means they can take away the introductory rate if you're a day late. Also, take note of the penalty APR and when it is applied. If you trigger the penalty rate, you could also be saying goodbye to your introductory rate.

You've picked the right card

You are now ready to apply. You can do this online or via the mail if you've received an offer in your mailbox. Some online applications allow you to request the balance transfer while you're filling it out. Other applications require that you get approved for the card first and then you can make the request.

If you have more than one credit card balance that you want to transfer, list them in priority order. You might not get a credit limit that's large enough to transfer all of your balances. So list the balance that's costing you the most first and so on.

You might have to pay off a balance or two at a time if your credit limit is too small. You can always call the issuer and ask them to reconsider the limit. In fact, I encourage you to do so if you can make a compelling case. You just never know.

When your balance transfer becomes a nightmare

I guess you noticed that I'm focusing on mistakes and how to avoid them in this book. One reason is because I've noticed that mistakes get people's attention. Sometimes it's much easier just to know what you should *never* do, especially if you hear about the consequences. And when it comes to credit cards, the results of negative consequences can be painful—sometimes even rage-inducing or humiliating.

So, in the spirit of saving you from a nightmarish balance transfer, I give you the seven biggest mistakes people make with them. They're not in any particular order because they're all bad.

Before you wave these away with a condescending smirk that would make *The Big Bang Theory's* Sheldon Cooper proud, though, you should know that people make these mistakes every day. And a lot of them are smarter than you and me. It's one of those "You don't know what you don't know" things. And what you don't know can cost you plenty.

Balance transfer nightmare #1: You used the card for new purchases. It's really difficult to get out of credit card debt. I mean, really, truly, ridiculously hard to get out of it. It just takes so much self-control, patience, and persistence. And did I mention self-control?

Once you start making new purchases with your balance transfer card, you're falling down the rabbit's hole. When you finally land, you'll still have your old debt. To further the nightmare metaphor, you'll also have a fresh layer of new debt on top of the old debt.

Sometimes this is the result of a misconception about the introductory rate for the balance transfer. I can see how you could mistakenly think that the offer extends to new purchases, especially if there are rewards to be had. This is how some folks end up with more debt. They find out later that they're being charged a 14.99 percent APR for the new tires on the truck.

Another way you can get into trouble is if you get a balance transfer card that actually *does* have an introductory rate for purchases. You think it is okay to use the card because you don't have to pay interest. But you weren't counting on your wife losing her job. Or maybe you were surprised that your son's travel baseball cost so much money. (I can vouch for this last one. Travel baseball costs a lot of money.)

Whatever the cause, you used the funds to pay for your family's immediate needs and you can't pay off the balance that includes the new purchases. And here it is, a year later, and the old and new debts have co-mingled into one big ugly debt.

Balance transfer nightmare #2: You let the expiration date for the introductory period sneak up on you. Okay, you know where you're supposed to look for the details of the offer. Right now, zero percent introductory offers range from six to 18 months, but they sometimes sneak up to 21 months for great customers.

Remember, you're supposed to figure out how much you have to pay each month to pay off your debt. Take it a step further and give yourself a halfway-to-freedom checkup. If your introductory period lasts 12 months, then set up a reminder to check your progress in six months. Set it up on your smartphone or on your PC or Mac. Or, if you love wall calendars, write it on the appropriate date.

If you don't pay off your balance, you'll have to start paying interest on it at the go-to rate. The go-to rate is the purchase APR that you'll pay when the introductory rate ends. And this leads us into the next mistake.

Balance transfer nightmare #3: You don't think you have to make monthly payments during the introductory period. It would be easy to assume that you don't have to make monthly payments on your debt. However, you have a zero percent APR for a period of time, not a free lunch. This is like any other balance, and you'd better make the payments or you're in default. This leads us right into nightmare #4.

Balance transfer nightmare #4: You make a late payment and lose the introductory rate. We talked about this a little bit when we discussed the fine print for balance transfers. Some issuers won't do this unless you're more than 60 days late. You have to read the fine print for your card to know what the triggers are. You could get stuck with a penalty rate, which can be as high as 29.99 percent. Plus, you could get hit with a late payment fee.

Some cards have done away with the penalty rate, but you'd still end up with the purchase APR applied to your balance. In other words, you're right back where you started. Even if it's a better APR, you missed a golden opportunity to pay off your debt without the interest charges.

Set up e-mail or text reminders so you never forget to pay your bill. Or you can set up an automatic payment in the amount you decided to pay every month to pay the balance off before the introductory period ends.

Balance transfer nightmare #5: You thought cash advances were included in the introductory rate. This is similar to making the assumption that purchases are included in the introductory offer. And I can see how it could happen. Unless you see a statement in the fine print that specifies that cash advances are included, assume they are not. In fact, I don't think I've seen a situation where cash advances have been included.

Credit card companies make a lot of money on cash advances. There isn't a grace period, so the interest starts accruing as soon as the transaction is posted to your account. So it's not surprising that issuers wouldn't want to cut into that source of revenue. If you get a cash advance, you have a special APR for that. And it's usually pretty high, like a 24 or 25 percent APR.

Balance transfer nightmare #6: You stop making payments on your old card too soon. This one is a shame because it could be easily avoided. I went over the follow-up steps earlier in this chapter but, just to reinforce the idea, I'll say it again here.

You have to keep making payments to your old bank until your new bank tells you that the transfer is complete. And even then, follow up with your old bank to confirm it on their end. Check your online account to prove to yourself that it's zero.

Balance transfer nightmare #7: You close your old account and don't realize it affects your score. The impact of closing one account depends on a couple of factors. If it's an account you've had for many years, it will eventually have a negative impact on your FICO. Closed accounts can stay on your credit report for up to 10 years, so the impact shouldn't happen right away.

The bigger issue is your utilization ratio. You'll lose that available credit you had on the card you closed. We've already talked about credit utilization ratios, but it's worth reviewing again because a lot of folks think they should close their old credit card once the balance transfer is complete.

Here's an example. Your credit cards: Card A, Card B, and Card C, which you just opened to make a balance transfer. Each card has a $3,000 credit limit. Card A had a $2,500 balance, so you opened Card C and transferred the balance to that account.

Your ratio: $2,500 / $9,000 = .2777 = 27.8 percent ratio, which is less than 30 percent, so it's fine.

You close Card A and this is your new ratio: $2,500 / $6,000 = .4166 = 41.7 percent, which is no longer fine. This part of the FICO score is no longer optimized.

If you're planning to refinance your mortgage or apply for any kind of loan, this could have a negative impact. Having a lower score does more than help you get the best credit cards. It helps you get lower rates on mortgages, health insurance, life insurance, and auto insurance.

So unless you have a problem with compulsive spending, I recommend keeping the account open. But if you're in a place where you feel your only chance of staying out of debt is to close your credit card accounts, then that's what you should do.

Life after debt

Getting and staying out of debt is essential to your well-being and happiness. It's been decades since I got out of debt, but I still remember how it felt when I achieved a debt-free status. Here are just a few things you can look forward to:

- ◆ You will have more physical and mental energy because you aren't being weighed down with your debt.
- ◆ You will feel more confident because you're in control of your present and your future.
- ◆ Your self-esteem will grow because you faced a big hurdle and overcame it.
- ◆ You don't judge others. You now have empathy, and this makes you a better friend and partner, and this strangely gives you even more peace of mind.

- You can build a savings account and save for something you really want.
- You're more creative than you've ever been in your life, and this translates into your personal and professional life.

At the beginning of this chapter, we talked about how heavy debt feels. As you begin paying down your debt, you'll begin to feel lighter. You'll feel a momentum that will help you keep going. Embrace the momentum and ride that wave all the way to financial freedom.

10

Seven Ways to Use a Credit Card to Rebuild Credit

know how awful it feels when you have a bad credit history. Take comfort, however, in knowing that you can do something about it. Even if you're still in credit card debt, there are some steps you can take to help your credit score go up inch by inch. You need patience, though, because your history didn't get ruined in one day. But with persistence and willpower, you can improve your credit history over time.

No one can give you a timetable because it's a very individual thing. Depending on the specifics in your credit file, it could take less than a year or much longer than a year. Turning bad credit into a good credit history is an organic process. Give it time to evolve naturally and it will happen.

That's why when someone says they can fix your credit in 48 hours, they're lying through their teeth. So before we jump into the legitimate ways to rebuild your credit, there are a few things you should know about the credit repair industry so you can protect yourself from fraudsters.

Are credit repair companies scams?

We've all seen the ads. Bankruptcy? No problem! Collection accounts? Easy to fix! The Acme Credit Repair Company will make all the bad stuff disappear from your credit file—for a fee, of course.

I know it's easy to fall for these scams because you just want your good credit back. And these companies know that, so they prey on your vulnerability. These companies will even promise you a new credit identity.

How do they do it? They often sell social security numbers. According to the Federal Trade Commission (FTC), if you apply for credit with an illegal social security number, you're committing a crime. In fact, it's fraud if you lie on a credit card application. You're dealing with a credit repair scam if any of the following are true:

- They tell you they can create a new credit identity.
- They guarantee they can move negative information from your credit report.
- They tell you to dispute information on your credit report even if you tell them it's accurate.
- They tell you to lie on a credit application.
- They want their money up-front before they do any work on your behalf.
- They seem incapable of explaining your legal rights.

Scam artists get more creative every day, so this isn't a complete list. But you get the gist of it, right? Fortunately, you can take care of business all by yourself. If you'd like more information about this, you can write to the Federal Trade Commission, Sixth and Pennsylvania Avenues, N.W., Washington, DC 20004 and request a brochure titled "Credit Repair: Self Help May Be Best."

Seven simple credit rebuilding strategies

Now that you know there isn't a quick fix, you're ready to get down to business. And by the way, if you're brand new to credit, most of these strategies will also help you establish a credit history.

I give to you seven—count 'em!—7 ways to rebuild your credit. As we've discussed, depending on how bad things are, it could take years. If you have credit card debt, that also slows down your progress. But the sooner you start working on the rebuilding process, the sooner you'll get there.

Strategy #1: Get a secured credit card

You know how all the very best cards require excellent credit? Well, there are some credit cards out there that are a bit forgiving. Now, you have to be careful. There are predatory lenders that try to take advantage of folks who are desperate for a credit card. There are some decent cards for those with fair credit scores, but once you drop below 620, it's downright scary.

Some of the unsecured credit cards for bad credit can have interest rates higher than 35 percent. In 2010, First Premier offered a credit card that had a jaw-dropping 79.9 percent APR. The issuer eventually dropped that card, but those of us who follow the credit card industry will never forget it.

Another problem with unsecured credit cards for the subprime category is the fees. There can be application fees or maintenance fees. So instead of getting an unsecured credit card that targets those with bad credit, think about getting a secured card. The reason is that secured credit cards often have much better terms.

If your credit score is in the toilet and you're psychologically ready to rebuild, a secured credit card is a useful tool. But don't do this if your problem stems from out-of-control spending. The right secured credit card can rebuild your credit history, but if you don't use the card responsibly, you'll end up worse off than ever.

Here's how it works. You make a deposit into a bank account and that "secures" the card for you. The card issuer gives you a credit card and you use the card just like a regular credit card. It doesn't say "secured" on the card, so there's no stigma attached to it. As long as you choose a secured card that reports to all three major credit bureaus, you'll be able to use the card to build credit. But this is the key ingredient: *The credit card issuer must report your payment history to all three major credit bureaus.*

As I've already mentioned, to help you choose the best card you can qualify for, I have a best-to-worst list on my Website of more than 20 secured credit cards. Each secured card on the list is also linked to one of my neurotically thorough card reviews. And if you're by any chance associated with the military, there are some very good secured cards available to you.

You might be wondering if secured credit cards will show up on your credit report as a "secured" card. Sometimes it will be labeled as a secured credit card, but sometimes it will appear on your report as just another unsecured credit card. It totally depends on the issuer.

First Progress offers three secured credit cards and they are reported to the bureaus as "unsecured." But Citi, which offers one of the best secured cards, reports to the bureaus as "secured."

Does it look bad if it's reported as secured? It's not ideal, but I wouldn't spend much time worrying about how it's reported. Your focus right now has to be on using the card to rebuild your credit. Improving your credit history and your credit score is the name of the game here.

You should know that the FICO score doesn't differentiate between secured and unsecured. Your payment history and utilization ratio are included in the score calculation as if it's unsecured. Really, it doesn't matter one whit. Your payment history and all-around responsible financial behavior are what matter. So don't sweat the details. Focus all of the positive energy you can muster on the big picture. Think about how proud you'll be when your score gets up into the "fair" range.

Some issuers that offer secured cards also have unsecured credit cards. Some banks, such as Wells Fargo, state that if you use your secured card responsibly you could "graduate" to one their unsecured cards. How long does it take to graduate? It varies, of course, but you should count on using the secured card for about 12 to 18 months.

Strategy #2: Don't apply for a lot of cards at one time

In Chapter 1, do you remember what my first big mistake was? It was applying for every credit card offer. At the time, I had no idea I was trashing my credit score (or what was left of it) by applying for every card offer I got in the mail.

I know it might make sense to you that the more credit you have, the better your score will be. But sometimes, it's the opposite. Every time you apply for a card, you get hit with a "hard inquiry" on your credit file.

In general, I think people get too uptight about one or two hard inquiries. Sure, your score might drop from two to five points for each inquiry, even if you get turned down for the card. But if you apply for four cards in one week, you could do some serious damage to your score. That's an eight- to 20-point drop.

Some people, when trying to rebuild, go into panic mode. They tell themselves that they need several new credit cards to prove they're a good risk. Often, though, this approach backfires. In many cases, these individuals don't have good enough credit to get approved for the cards they're applying for. And when you have a low score already, you can't afford this approach. It's not the number of cards that will boost your credit; it's the responsible use of the cards, as well as the timely payment of all the other bills in your life.

If you think you need another card other than a secured card, try for a department store or a gas credit card. This is one of the few times I'll actually recommend a retail card. It's my understanding that a retail card doesn't give the same "oomph" as a card from a major bank will to your FICO score. But it does help a little. Also, retails cards are fairly easy to get. If you use them responsibly, it shows you've got credit and can manage it.

However, you have to be careful with these credit cards. They tend to have high APRs. I'm not going to pick on any one card because credit card terms, including APRs, change all the time. Seriously, though, around a 25 percent APR is not unusual. Don't get a retail card unless you know you'll pay it off every month. Here's why: I've seen people rack up thousands of dollars on retail cards. Thousands! And when you're paying off debt at a 25 percent interest rate, you can get pretty depressed.

Strategy #3: Keep a low balance on your credit card

We've already talked about your credit utilization ratio. But just in case you're one of those readers who likes to read chapters out of order (no worries; I do that, too), I'll explain it again quickly. The utilization ratio is the amount of credit you have used compared to the amount you have available when you add up all of your credit limits. If you keep your ratio less than 30 percent, you're in good shape.

Here's an insider tip: Keep it less than 10 percent, and you'll maximize this part of your FICO score. Your utilization ratio accounts for 30 percent of your FICO score, so it's very important.

Further, when you're trying to rebuild your credit and pump up your score, keep your utilization ratio less than 10 percent on *each credit card*. If you're wondering if keeping it at zero would help, the answer is no. You actually do need to use your card and pay off the bill to prove you're creditworthy.

So, of course, you need to keep tabs on your credit card balances. I've already recommended using free online money management tools to track all of your spending. But you can also check your balances online whenever you want to. This has an added benefit: If you check your accounts frequently, you'll also be able to catch any signs of fraud in the early stages.

The Internet makes keeping control of your credit life much easier than it has ever been before. One of the reasons I got into massive debt was because I didn't keep track of my expenses. It felt like I was getting free stuff! But guess what? The bill would show up and I'd be shocked. My ratio was at 100 percent more than once.

Bonus tip: If you have credit card debt, after you've started paying down your balance, ask for a higher credit limit. This will decrease your utilization ratio and boost your score a little.

Strategy #4: Pay your balance in full by the due date every month

If you don't pay the balance in full, you'll pay interest expense. This means your balance gets bigger and bigger due to an unpleasant thing called compound interest. So that's one reason right there not to carry a balance. But another reason is that paying your bill off every month makes you look very responsible. Keep your balance low and this shouldn't be difficult to do.

Also, keep in mind that you can change your due date if it isn't in sync with your cash flow. Lately, I'm seeing credit cards tout this option as if it's a break-through feature. However, you've always had the power to call and ask for this, and most issuers oblige.

Let's say your due date is now at an optimal time. If you are using a tool like Mint.com, you can set up payment reminders. Often, your credit card issuer will offer a service that allows you to set up reminders via e-mail or text. One late payment can wreck your score. The amount of wreckage depends on your current score. The higher your score, the harder you'll fall.

What if you get into a jam? This happens to all of us. Life is messy and unpredictable things happen. Your budget now becomes your friend. Search your budget and find ways to decrease expenses in other areas. If you can't pay your bill for whatever reason, call your issuer and have a heart-to-heart talk.

Have your story ready. Be charming. If you don't know how to be charming, just be polite. Banks really aren't as evil as they're portrayed. Sure, they're sneaky, but they understand that you're a customer. Without customers, they don't make money. You might be surprised at the help you'll receive. Maybe they can decrease your minimum for one month. Or if things are really bad, you might qualify for their hardship program. Most credit card issuers have these, but they aren't publicized.

Asking for a break doesn't always work, but when you're in control of your financial life, you take the bull by the horns and try to make things better for yourself. As one famous British philosopher once said, "You don't always get what you want, but if you try sometimes, you just might find, you get what you need."

Strategy #5: Don't close unused credit cards

Earlier, I said not to open too many credit card accounts. It's also important not to close credit card accounts that you currently have. We've covered this in enough detail for you to know that "the less credit I have, the better I look" argument is incorrect.

Here's the problem, though: When you close an account, you lose the available credit associated with that card. Remember the utilization ratio that I explained in Strategy #3? Well, if you decrease the amount of credit you have available, the result is that your ratio goes up. When your ratio goes up, your FICO score usually goes down. So we want your ratio to be low—less than 10 percent. Therefore, unless the account has a huge annual fee or some other objectionable fee, try to keep it open.

Another issue that's brought up a lot whenever this topic is discussed is that you lose the history associated with that account. Closed accounts don't drop off your credit report right away. In fact, they can stay on your history for up to 10 years.

The main issue is the loss of available credit. Like all things in life, there are exceptions. As a rule, though, you don't want to close your accounts, especially when your overall objective is to improve your history and improve your score.

Strategy #6: Become an authorized user

We talked about this in Chapter 5 as a strategy for building credit. This is also a strategy for repairing your credit if you can't get approved for a card on your own. As well, this is a good strategy to do in combination with other strategies. For example, get a secured card and become an authorized user on a credit card.

You can benefit from someone else's good credit by becoming an authorized user on their credit card account. The key, of course, is to choose an account holder who has great credit and who's willing to let you become an authorized user. The downside is that your credit can temporarily get worse if the account holder doesn't pay the credit card bill on time or racks up debt. So choose your account holder carefully.

Strategy #7: Get a cosigner

This can be a good strategy to help you rebuild your credit, but it's fraught with landmines. It can be a legal quagmire if things don't go as planned. When you get a cosigner, this means you're both legally liable for any credit card debt. So be careful that the person you choose as a cosigner is very responsible. Otherwise, this could have the opposite effect of what you're looking for.

If your cosigner goes crazy with the credit card, you're stuck with the bill if he doesn't pay. If the bill isn't paid on time, then your dreams of rebuilding your credit history goes down the tubes. You then have to start over again.

You must have a heart-to-heart talk with your potential cosigner before you make the leap to become joint owners on an account, just to make sure you're both on the same page. I've seen relationships go awry because this talk never took place.

If your cosigner has good enough credit for you to get a decent credit card with good terms, that's great. If you go this route, communicate often with each other. Determine who is paying the bill each month. If you and your cosigner use the card responsibly, then you're on your way to better credit.

11

Exreme Credit: Strategies for the Power User

asten your seat belts because this can be a bumpy ride. You must have excellent credit to get on this ride. Keep your arms and legs (and FICO score) inside the ride at all times. If at any point during the ride you start feeling sick (or in debt), then get off immediately and seek help from a credit expert.

What's extreme credit? It's a name I made up for credit-card-related activities that involve a high degree of risk. These activities include: credit card arbitrage, travel hacking, buying hundreds of dollars worth of gift cards to take advantage of cash-back offers, and financing a large expense using a zero percent introductory APR for purchases. And this is just the stuff I know about. Human beings are smart and creative. Really, nothing would surprise me when it comes to rewards hacking.

You shouldn't try any of the strategies we're going to talk about in this chapter unless *all* of the following are true:

◆ You have an excellent FICO score and credit history.

- ◆ You're not planning to apply for credit any time soon.
- ◆ You're organized with your finances and you pay your bills on time.
- ◆ You have an emergency fund just in case something goes terribly wrong.
- ◆ You don't have debt other than your mortgage, which is good debt.
- ◆ You have a steady source of income.
- ◆ You enjoy taking financial risk. It doesn't matter if you enjoy bungee jumping. Financial risk is different.
- ◆ You're older than 55, but you have a comfortable nest egg for your golden years.

In other words, this isn't an activity I'd recommend for anyone who is unemployed, risk averse, or doesn't have a rainy day fund. There's actually one more factor to consider. If you've had problems with gambling, you might want to steer clear of extreme credit. It's really important to keep a cool head and not overdo it.

Credit score warning

It can be quite a thrill to take chances and then profit from it. I mentioned that you need excellent credit to play these games. Now, when you're in the midst of the some of these extreme credit activities, your credit scores are going to be bobbing up and down.

You might say it doesn't matter because you're not refinancing any time soon. You don't need a car loan. In fact, you have no credit needs at the moment and when you do, you'll stop playing.

Just please keep in mind that your credit score is more than a number that helps you get the best credit cards. Your score is also considered when you get health insurance, life insurance, car insurance, and more. The better credit you have, the less you pay for some of life's necessary expenses.

Credit card arbitrage

Arbitrage in its purest form is buying a security at a low price and immediately selling it on a different market at a higher price. For example, you buy a dozen old Pink Floyd albums for pennies at a garage sale and then you turn around and sell them on eBay for $25 each.

Here's how it works with credit cards:

1. You apply for a zero-percent interest balance transfer card.

2. You then deposit the money in a high-yield savings account or other short-term investment.

3. You make minimum payments on the card and you make them on time. (This is very important so you don't lose the zero percent rate.)

4. When the zero percent offer expires, you pay off the balance with the money from your savings account, CD, or whatever you invested the money in.

The money you have left over is your profit. Congratulations! Obviously, the more money you transfer, the more profit you'll make. Also, remember that you have to consider the transfer fee, which is usually 3 percent.

I've talked with people who have practiced arbitrage at astoundingly high dollar amounts. If you can get the credit limits and have the patience to track the due dates and payments, then more power to you. I honestly don't have the patience for this. However, I'm totally impressed with savvy consumers who can pull this off and make big profits.

Five to seven years ago, arbitrage was more prevalent. You could have savings accounts at 4 to 6 percent interest annually. Today, rates on savings accounts and CDs are lower. So you do have to be a little more creative these days and do your research to find a profitable place to park your cash. But it's still a good time to use a cousin of credit card arbitrage. If you have credit card debt, you can play the system and transfer your way out of debt.

Balance transfer your way out of debt

I covered the basics of balance transfers in Chapter 9. If you're in serious debt, though—say, more than $10,000—you might need to do multiple transfers to pay it off. It's tedious, but here's an example: you have $20,000 in credit card debt. You have $6,000 on Card A and $14,000 on Card B.

1. You apply for a zero-percent interest balance transfer card with an 18-month zero percent introductory rate.

2. If the limit is less than $20,000, call the issuer and say that you'd like to transfer more money. This often works if you have excellent credit.

3. You transfer $20,000 from Card A and Card B onto your new transfer card, which we'll call Card C.

4. You make minimum payments on Card C and you make them on time. (This is very important so you don't lose the zero percent rate.)

5. After 18 months, the introductory rate expires. You still owe $10,000.

6. You apply for a new balance transfer card, Card D, which has a 12-month introductory offer.

7. You transfer the $10,000 from Card C to Card D.

8. After 12 months, your debt is paid off! But if it isn't, you start the process again and transfer the remaining balance to a new transfer card, which, in our example, is now Card E. When the zero percent offer expires, you pay off the balance with the money from your savings account, CD, or whatever you invested the money in.

The rebel in me loves the idea of turning the tables on the credit card issuers. But take note of these do's and don'ts so you don't mess it up:

◆ Don't make a late payment or you're screwed.

◆ Don't make new purchases. Do you hear me? Don't do it.

◆ Don't make balance transfers to business credit cards because they aren't covered by the CARD Act. Too many things can go wrong.

◆ Do ask to have the transfer fee waived. It doesn't hurt to ask.

Travel hacking and bonus hopping

Travel hackers are relentless in their pursuit of miles, rewards points, the next status level, and anything travel-related that they can get for free or drastically reduced. True travel hackers rarely pay for travel. They get free tickets and free hotel stays, and know how to take advantage of frequent flyer programs.

Obviously, you need to be very organized and savvy to do this. But before you get a card in this specialized area, come to my Website and read my review. You don't want to get stuck with a lemon.

Bonus hopping is another strategy that can be used to earn miles, points, or cash back. You know, whatever your heart desires! Here's a basic example: You get an offer for an airline card that has a 40,000 mile bonus offer if you spend $3,000 within the first three months.

You're thinking that you can rack up $3,000 in no time, so you get the card and earn your bonus. Months later, another offer shows up. This cash back card offers a $150 bonus if you spend $1,000 within the next three months. You go for it. Ka-ching! You've earned a free airline ticket and pocketed $150 within a few months and all you did was get some new cards with sign-up bonuses.

Here's another approach that kicks it up a notch: You apply for three cards at one time. You get a 40,000-mile bonus, which is worth $400, and 40,000 bonus points, which, in this case, is worth $500. You also apply for a cash back card with a $150 cash back bonus. But you have to spend $3,000 on each of the travel cards within the next three months to get the bonus. So that's $6,000. Now, add the cash back card requirement, which is $1,000.

You're now looking at $7,000 to spend within the next three months to get the bonuses. If you can do this without panicking and buying stuff you don't need just to reach the $7,000, then that's fine. However, don't underestimate the amount of time it takes to track all of this and make sure you spend the money wisely.

I also want to point out a common misconception that many consumers have shared with me. Many were under the impression that, if they applied for several credit cards on the same day, the FICO score algorithm would treat the multiple inquiries as if it was just one hard inquiry.

So they were surprised when their score dropped more than just a few points. I can understand why this is assumed. When you're looking for a mortgage and you make several applications within a few days, the score "understands" that you are rate shopping and treats the multiple inquires on your credit report as one hard inquiry.

The score, though, doesn't take this into consideration with credit card applications. Each time you apply for a credit card and the issuer looks at your credit report, the FICO score counts it as a hard inquiry. You already know that the impact on your score varies based on the details of your credit history. But generally, you can count a reduction of two to five points for *each* inquiry.

Therefore, applying for three cards could decrease your score by six to 15 points. On the other hand, if you received high credit limits, the increase in your available credit could offset this and, in some cases, even increase your score.

Now, if you start closing accounts as you open new ones, this is another issue because then you're losing available credit. So just remember that you're playing roulette with your score when you do this.

You can't predict how it will impact your score and you can't predict how long it will take to rebound. To be safe, allow six months to get your score settled if you're planning to apply for a mortgage, car loan, or a personal loan. Let me be clear: People do this and they often succeed. But I hesitate to recommend this to anyone who isn't really organized.

Credit card issuers are on to this

This is usually called "churning," but that sounds unpleasant, so I renamed it "bonus hopping." Some bloggers who specialize in travel hacking say to wait at least a business quarter between applications for new cards. I've done this kind of churning myself, but I spread it out for at least six months. If you do a lot of this, issuers catch on and they don't like it.

Credit card agreements usually spell out in plain language how the bonus offer is for first-time cardholders only. How many other things are stated clearly in these agreements? It's like this is the one thing they want to make absolutely sure you understand!

This used to be an issue because people would close accounts and then later, apply again and get the bonus—again. I've talked with several folks who had closed an account a few years earlier and, when they applied again, got approved but didn't receive the bonus. I guess they just wanted to see if they could slip through the system.

Rewards padding

Several years ago, consumers figured out they could buy dollar coins with their rewards credit cards. The Presidential $1 Coin Act of 2005 was supposed to encourage the circulation of dollar coins.

Citizens were allowed to buy directly from the Mint's Website and, yes, they accepted credit cards. To top it off, shipping was free!

I'll bet you've already put the pieces together. Cardholders bought the coins and then deposited the coins in the bank. With that money, they paid off the credit card bill. The whole plan was designed to pad rewards points. It actually worked very well for many frequent flyers until the practice got a lot of press. Eventually, the Mint shut down the program.

Another rewards-padding technique is gobbling up gift cards. Remember the story about consumers buying up gift cards at grocery stores because they received 6 percent cash back if they used their Blue Cash Preferred Card? You can actually still do that with this card, but you're now capped at $6,000.

You can also buy gift cards with airline miles cards. Often, the shopping portals of the major credit cards give you extra rewards per dollar when you purchase items. Use this strategically, like for birthdays and during the holidays. Here are a few more ideas for padding statistics: pay taxes, pay tuition, pay for major appliances, and make car payments with rewards cards.

Another popular technique is to open a prepaid card account and buy reload cards with your rewards card. The reload cards are used to fund the prepaid card. Each reload card is about four or five dollars. If you have a rewards card where you get extra points at drug stores, you can earn rewards in a hurry. Prepaid cards have fees, so you have to know what you're doing.

Travel rewards cards are often popular for these maneuvers, but some cash back cards also sometimes have a drugstore category where you get 5 percent cash back for three months.

It's also possible to use a zero percent introductory purchase APR card for major purchases. I have a friend who once bought her son a car using this method. She had excellent credit and got a credit card with a 12-month introductory offer. She paid off the card in 12 months and paid zero interest. She basically used the introductory offer as a loan. Car loans are pretty cheap right now, but you never know when that will change.

What if this backfires and you can't pay the balance off? You can then get a balance transfer credit card. You transfer the remainder of the car balance to the balance transfer card. This type of strategy is nice to have around when you need something big and you want to finance it interest-free.

Common mistakes to avoid

Here I go again, wanting to tell you about mistakes. Well, it seems easier to remember what *not* to do. I've already given you the talk about who should not be participating in extreme credit activities. So here's a list of the most common mistakes I see and hear about the various forms of hacking:

- Getting so focused on earning miles that you lose sight of how much you're spending.

- Paying more than you have to for something just because the place where you're buying gives you more miles. Run the numbers and make sure you're making a profit.

- Not having a method in place to help you keep track of the rewards and the bonus dates and requirements.

- Having so many cards with sign-up bonuses that you can't meet the spending requirements on time.

- Closing accounts after you've earned the bonus. Instead, if the card has an annual fee, ask to be downgraded to a version that doesn't have the fee.

- Opening up so many credit cards that you can't manage the details even though you're using a Website for tracking.

Travel hacking without using credit cards

There are ways to travel hack without using credit cards. So if at any point you're uncomfortable with extreme credit, check out other strategies. There are Websites designed for this, too. (I think there's a Website for everything.)

All kinds of vendors promote partnerships with travel-related merchants from time to time. You can often find details on the rewards program or frequent flyer program you're in. For example, if you're a SkyMiles member, you can earn miles by renting your car at Hertz on a trip. Often you'll find limited time offers where you can really boost the miles earned.

Sometimes the vendor will be unrelated. At the time I was researching this book, SunTrust Bank was offering a Delta debit card. This is rare because there are very few debit rewards programs. You earn miles for everyday debit use, whether it's groceries or gas. You can also earn miles dining at specific restaurants. United has a Mileage Plus Dining program, for example, where you can earn up to five points per dollar spent.

Some people feel that some hackers go too far. I have to agree that if you take a hacking strategy far enough to ruin a good thing for the masses, then you've gone too far.

I still mourn the loss of the unlimited 6 percent grocery rewards on the Blue Cash Preferred. My feeling is this: make a profit, but don't get too greedy. Once you start playing a system to the maximum, it goes away and then everyone loses out because the economics will no longer make it sustainable for the issuer.

There's that sweet spot where we can all make a buck, but we don't want to destroy the opportunity to have a great rewards program on a particular card. So on that final thought, go forth and hack!

12

Hot Credit Card Trends to Watch

How do I spot trends? Not by asking bank executives, that's for sure. They'll tell you what they *want* you to know. It's a marketing game. If they're creating something exotic— for example, a credit card that talks to you while you're in the store—they will not want their competitors to know about it. Hey, I don't blame them.

I spot trends by reading *everything* I can get my hands on that has to do with credit cards and credit scores. I read white papers, review statistics from the Federal Reserve, read the reports from the U.S. Bureau of Economic Analysis, talk to vendors who are on the fringe of the industry, read reports from payment processors, read the newsletter of the National Retail Federation to spot consumer trends, read press releases from the credit bureaus, and follow market research firms, such as Mintel. Didn't I tell you I had an exciting life?

On the more enjoyable side, I also follow finance journalists and personal finance bloggers. I never miss Liz Weston's

MSN Money column. I also enjoy listening to Gerri Detweiler's *Talk Credit Radio Show*.

I use a variety of sources for my information. I've followed this industry for a long time, so I can see subtle changes when they occur. I'm the first to admit that sometimes I'm right and sometimes I'm not. However, I'm right more often than I'm wrong (if I do say so myself).

Credit cards are easier to get

It's been a tough road for those who have credit scores less than 700, and especially less than 650. Even when the recession was at its worst, consumers with excellent credit were sought after by the banks. The economy had sputtered a lot during this recovery, but I think there's reason for optimism. The banks think so, too.

Credit cards are going to be easier to get for both small business owners and consumers. As I mentioned in Chapter 8 about business credit cards, banks feel optimistic that credit is getting looser. Small business has had a rough time of it in recent years, so this is good news for them and for the overall economy.

I like this trend, but if you're getting a business credit card, remember what I said about the CARD Act. Business credit cards are not covered by the Act, so pay attention to your mail and don't carry a balance if you can help it.

As for consumers, I'm seeing APR ranges widen ever so slightly. Remember how some credit cards have ranges instead of just one APR? Let's say the APR range is 12.99 percent to 19.99 percent. I've seen ranges change on the high end and on the low end recently.

This means that the underwriting (the process of evaluating a customer for a credit card) is loosening up. They might start considering folks with good credit, say 710, for a credit card that usually requires a 740 score. By increasing the top of the range, the issuer can bring in riskier customers and limit their risk by giving them a 20.99 percent APR. If you don't carry a balance, of course, interest rates don't matter.

One thing to be concerned about when it comes to easy credit is the impact on consumers who have far less-than-perfect credit. These folks have been able to get credit cards again. This has a habit of bringing out predatory lenders. So if you're in rebuilding mode, be careful about signing up for a new credit card. Read the fine print carefully—and then read it again.

Remember that sometimes it's better to stick with a secured credit card than to get an unsecured credit card with a high APR and fees. I'm seeing a few new secured credit cards on the market and I think that's awesome. For a while, there wasn't a lot of good competition. People who are working hard to rebuild credit deserve excellent products to help them succeed.

Also, have you ever noticed that just about every time you read about credit card predictions, you see something about sign-up bonuses?

This is the low-hanging fruit of the credit card prediction business. So I'll pile on too! Don't get me wrong: The value of the bonuses go up and down. It's kind of cyclical, but with the exception of the worst recession years, there's usually one time during the year that the bonuses look very good indeed.

Credit card apps for smartphones

I'm not a natural-born techie. But I'll admit that I'm totally fascinated with the intersection of credit cards and technology. This is a trend that I think is particularly cool. There are some solid players in the space already, but the features are continually evolving as the market needs are being sorted out. If you enjoy using your smart phone and being on the leading edge of an evolving product, then these apps are for you. Here are a few smartphone apps to check out.

Wisely. Wisely is still a work-in-progress, but I like what I hear about it. This app helps you stretch your money further. There's a budgeting feature, so it helps you see the big picture when you make purchases. This app also helps you decide which credit card to use to maximize your rewards.

Website: *Wise.ly*

Platforms: iPhone only at this time. But an Android version is in the works.

Reward Summit. This app tells you the best credit card to use for a given purchase based on your location and rewards program. It even recommends new cards based on your actual usage patterns over time. And now there's a Reward Summit extension for Chrome.

Website: *RewardSummit.com.*

Platforms: iPhone and Android versions.

Smorecard. This app also helps you pick the best rewards card when making purchases. It takes a more direct route, though. You don't give your account information. You just select the credit cards that you have. You can also customize your credit card profiles so introductory offers and special rewards are considered.

Website: *Smorecard.com.*

Platforms: iPhone and Android versions.

Banks get more engaged in social media

Credit card mailings are still a popular way to solicit new customers, but according to Mintel, the number of mass mailings has decreased a little. It's too soon to know exactly what's going on, but it's possible that banks are turning more to social media, especially Facebook. It's a brilliant move from the bank's perspective. Think of all the consumer behavior data they can collect. And talk about target advertising!

You know all those ads that run down the right side of the Facebook page? I noticed that the social media site was running a lot of ads for credit repair. Just to mess with Facebook, I started Googling "Coach handbags." Now, I've never spent more than $30 on a purse, but I've walked past a Coach store at the mall. After I did this, I started seeing ads for Coach handbags on Facebook. I have to say, these bags are gorgeous. It's a good thing I'm a tightwad or I'd totally buy one.

My point is that when you're on social media, like Facebook, credit cards issuers have a golden opportunity to interact with you. They can come across like they're, well, human. Some issuers have a separate Facebook page for their most popular cards. Expect to see the banks ramp up their social media presence even more. If you post about needing a new cash back card, expect to see the Chase Freedom Visa pop up in your ad space.

As for the credit card Facebook pages, this is a good way to maximize your benefit from the card. There are contests, updates about bonus rewards, and reminders about quarterly categories. This is also a great way to voice a complaint. It's public and they have to respond to you.

Indeed, you have new power with social media. I've "taken it to Twitter" several times when I couldn't get a response from an issuer the old-fashioned way (e-mail or a phone call).

Another good thing about this trend is that the credit bureaus do Twitter Chats and you have a chance to ask experts questions. For instance, Experian has a weekly TweetChat about credit (#CreditChat). A lot of experts show up and you get almost instant answers to your questions.

The next frontier for the credit card issuers is Google+. I've seen issuers there, but I expect banks to get even more involved. Google is everywhere and the banks know they need a presence on Google+. I'll bet that we will see a lot of Google+ Hangouts by the card issuers.

Prepaid cards keep growing

I mentioned prepaid cards earlier, but this is a trend that's continuing so I want to make sure that I cover it properly. I'll be honest and say that I'm not a fan of prepaid cards. There are only a few that I would recommend. The reason is high fees and less-than-transparent disclosure statements. Frankly, I think it's crazy to have to pay to spend your own money.

Prepaid cards first started gaining momentum when the Durbin Amendment capped the interchange fees on debit cards. The banks lost a bundle (over $9 billion in annual revenue) over this. Sometimes legislation is a good thing. However, sometimes it causes unintended negative consequences, which is what happened when the Durbin Amendment was passed.

First, we saw a reduction in checking accounts with rewards. Then some checking accounts started charging fees. Prepaid cards are not covered by the Durbin Amendment, so this helped propel these cards to popularity.

To replace the debit card income stream, many banks are issuing prepaid cards. These cards are unregulated and they aren't subject to the restrictions of the Durbin Amendment. I do think that the Consumer Financial Protection Bureau will take a look at these cards and the sooner the better.

One of the reasons I'm including prepaid cards in a book about credit cards is that there's a frequent misconception that you can build credit with a prepaid card. It's confusing because you see logos, like Visa and MasterCard, on prepaid cards. This is just the payment network that the card issuer uses.

When you use prepaid cards, you're spending your own money. You're not using credit at all. And what further complicates this misconception is that a few celebrities have come out with cards and implied that you might be able to build credit with these cards. They make no promises, but because most people have a tenuous grasp on how credit works, they make the leap to believing they can build credit. If you want to build credit and you have a bad credit score, use a secured credit card.

I do understand that there's a group of folks who can't get a traditional checking account. Maybe you're in the Chex system or you have bad credit. If you must use a prepaid card, think of it as a short-term solution while you work toward getting back into a traditional bank or a credit union.

Now, I mentioned these cards have a lot of fees. Read the fine print for a prepaid card very carefully. And please, for the love of God, don't get your teen a prepaid card. Get your kid a free (or low-cost) checking account and a debit card.

One more thing I want you to know about prepaid cards. When people are asked why they prefer prepaid cards, they often say because they can't spend more money than they have. They even often say that they wish this was true with debit cards and their checking accounts.

Well, it *is* true. You can opt out of overdraft protection on your checking account. If you do this, your card will be rejected when you go over the amount of money in your account. The same is true for credit cards. With credit cards, you have to opt in to be allowed to go over your credit limit.

Prepaid cards will continue to grow, no doubt. I'm just doing my part here to encourage you not to use them and, if you must, do your research and choose a card that has limited fees.

Chip-and-signature credit cards

A lot of people get confused about this because there are also chip-and-PIN credit cards, which are used in Europe. Europe has used these cards for years because the fraud rates were so high. It's easy to clone the magnetic-stripe cards. Google Wallet seems to get all the press, but the United States has made great progress when it comes to credit cards that are embedded with computer chips.

I mentioned these when we were talking about the fine print because there are a few elite credit cards that are "smart cards."

Chip-and-signature credit cards are similar to chip-and-PIN cards, but there's no PIN required. Instead, these cards contain a computer chip that requires a signature.

One of the reasons that chip-and-signature cards are being pushed right now is because some Americans have been unable to use their magnetic-stripe credit cards when traveling in Europe. As I mentioned, Europe uses chip-and-PIN technology, so when Americans try to use their magnetic-stripe cards, they sometimes get denied unless the merchant has an old-fashioned swipe machine.

One point I want to make is that, in most cases, you can use your magstripe card. You might have to ask the person who's processing your purchase to do it manually. The real problem is when American travelers are in a location where there's no human being around, such as at a train station kiosk that requires a smart card. If you're concerned about having problems using a chip-and-signature credit card in America, then don't be. These cards also have magnetic stripes on the back.

So why is Europe ahead when it comes to smart cards? For one thing, it's very expensive for merchants to get the equipment necessary to process smart cards. But they now have incentive because Visa and MasterCard have told merchants to get the equipment necessary to process payments by 2015. Guess what happens if they don't have it in place by 2015? Visa and MasterCard plan to shift fraud liability to the merchants. Well, that ought to take care of any slackers.

Mobile wallets

I couldn't decide whether to call this mobile wallets or mobile payments. The terms are starting to be used together. Then there's also mobile banking. I think it's very cool that we can take a photo of a check with our phones to make a deposit. This is the ultimate convenience, right?

I think that Americans are slowly getting more comfortable with the idea of using something like Google Wallet, which uses near-field communication technology (NFC). I talk about this every year when I make predictions or discuss trends. I predict that it won't be embraced anytime soon, but that we'll slowly make progress to that end.

I'm making that prediction again because we're just not there. We'll keep talking about them because it gets a lot of press. There's a big difference between talking about what a cool idea it is and actually using mobile wallets. To be honest, I don't see the majority of consumers actually using mobile wallets for a few more years.

One of the issues is that we're not convinced it's entirely safe to have our financial life on our smartphones. I'm not saying that I believe they're not secure enough, by any means. I really don't know. It should be more secure because magstripe cards are so susceptible to fraud. I think time will tell and that's what a lot of folks are waiting for.

Here's another issue: Does it solve an actual problem? Is it that time consuming to whip out a piece of plastic and pay your bill? People don't change their behavior unless there's a compelling reason, like it's a huge time saver or much more secure.

This leads to another favorite headline that I frequently see: *Credit cards will soon be extinct!* Even when the time comes and we all shout, "Thank you, God, for Google Wallet!" we'll still have our plastic cards for backup. What if you're standing in line to buy something and your phone battery dies? I don't know about you, but my phone isn't my top priority. I work at home and sometimes I don't notice that my battery is almost dead unless I try to text my kids.

My bottom line on this issue is that the trend toward mobile payments and mobile wallets will continue. That train has left the station and I actually think there are many good things that come with it. But it's going to take more time for most Americans to get on that ride. That might be a good thing until all the kinks are worked out.

Zero percent balance transfer offers

I see really good balance transfer offers during the first few months of the New Year. Banks are pretty good at marketing their wares. Right after the holidays, people tend to be a little overextended. Many folks even have credit card debt because they went all out over the holiday season.

Like sign-up bonuses, zero percent balance transfer offers tend to be cyclical too. If the economy is going well, sometimes you'll see good offers during the summer months. This is also marketing strategy. People are paying off vacations that they couldn't afford to take.

I spent an entire chapter on balance transfers because they're big business for the banks. Let's say you transfer a $10,000 debt to one of their credit cards. The banks know that, in many cases, some of that balance will still be there when the introductory period ends. At that point, you start paying interest on that balance.

The banks play the numbers here. Many will pay it off completely, but there's a group who won't. The bank profits from those who don't. At the end of the day, though, they still have the new customers who paid off their debt during the introductory period. And these consumers might one day carry a balance and pay interest charges.

As the economy continues to improve, people will increase their use of credit cards. They'll start feeling confident about the future. They might even carry a balance. So I think balance transfer offers will be strong for the next few years. The longest zero percent balance transfer offer I see right now is 18 months, but I've been told by a consumer that he received a 21-month offer in the mail.

Banks don't like to be one-upped, so when one bank takes the leap, others often follow. They compete for customers so it's possible that we'll see longer introductory periods than we've seen in a while. Would you believe that a few years ago I saw an offer for

24 months? I'd be surprised if we see more than one or two cards offering that in the future, but if the economy looks good and consumer spending is high, then anything is possible.

Appendix: A Credit Card Glossary

Affinity card. This is a credit card that's usually offered through a partnership between an organization, such as a university, and a financial lending institution.

Annual fee. Some credit card companies charge an annual fee for the use of their card. The fee is usually billed to the consumer's credit card account. Annual fees range from zero up to almost $500 for elite cards.

Annual percentage rate (APR). The APR is the actual yearly cost of borrowing money. The APR includes fees and any additional costs.

Application fee. Some credit card issuers charge a fee to apply for a credit card. This is more common with credit cards for bad credit.

Authorized user. An authorized user is someone who has permission to use a credit card, but who isn't legally responsible for paying the bill or for any debt on the credit card.

Available credit. This is the difference between the amount of outstanding charges to a credit card and the account holder's credit limit. If you have a $1,000 credit limit and your outstanding charges are $200, then your available credit is $800.

Balance transfer. A balance transfer involves transferring credit card debt from one credit card account to a new credit card account that has a lower APR.

Balance-transfer fee. This fee is charged when you make a balance transfer. It's usually between 3 percent and 5 percent of the amount transferred.

Bankruptcy. When consumers or businesses can't pay their bills, they sometimes get legal help and declare bankruptcy. In a Chapter 7 bankruptcy, a consumer's debts (most of them, at least) are discharged. In a Chapter 11 bankruptcy, a business is allowed to restructure its debts. An individual can also file Chapter 11 if he or she meets certain requirements. In a Chapter 13 bankruptcy, a consumer's debts are restructured, not discharged. Then the debt is repaid over three to five years, under bankruptcy court supervision. A bankruptcy has a negative effect on credit scores.

Card member agreement. The card member agreement provides terms and conditions and other cost information about a credit card. It's considered a contract, but the credit card issuer can make changes as long as it meets the legal requirements for notification.

Cash advance. This is a cash loan from a credit card via an ATM, a bank withdrawal, or "convenience" checks. The interest rates tend to be high and the interest starts accruing right away.

Cash-advance fee. When you get a cash advance on a credit card, you're charged a transaction fee. The fee is usually between 3 percent and 5 percent.

Cosigner. A cosigner is a person who signs an agreement to pay off the debt of someone else if that person defaults. A cosigner is sometimes used when the person applying for credit has limited or bad credit. In this case, a lender might be more likely to take a chance on the individual because there's less risk to the lender. But the cosigner is legally responsible for the debt if the individual with bad credit defaults. There are some credit cards that do not allow cosigners.

Co-branded card. This is a credit card that's usually offered through a partnership between a retailer, such as an airline or department store, and a bank or financial lending institution.

Credit bureau. These companies are sometimes called credit reporting agencies. The bureau gathers information about your payment history credit, debt, and other aspects of your credit life. The three major consumer credit bureaus are Equifax, TransUnion, and Experian.

Credit card. This is a plastic card that allows you to make a purchase when you choose not to pay cash. Your card's terms and conditions and any additional features will be outlined in your credit card agreement.

Credit card agreement. This is a document that outlines the terms and conditions for using your credit card. It is your contract with your credit card company.

Credit counseling service. These companies employ credit counselors who will talk with you about your financial situation and discuss repayment options with you. They often try to negotiate with your creditors. They may charge a fee for their services, or they may offer some free services.

Credit history. Your credit history is viewed by lenders when you apply for credit. It's a record of your behavior when it comes to borrowing and repaying debt.

Credit limit. This refers to the maximum amount of money you can charge to your credit card. It's also referred to as a credit line.

Credit-limit-increase fee. Some credit cards, usually those for bad credit, might charge this fee if you're approved for an increase in your credit limit.

Credit report. This is a report that shows your history of debts, repayment behavior, available credit, and credit inquiries. It is sometimes referred to as your credit history. Your report is one the resources lenders use to make lending decisions and to set rates.

Credit score. This is a three-digit number that reflects how well you handle credit. The score is based on several factors, including payment history, credit utilization ratio, inquiries, types of credit you have, and the length of your credit history. Your score, usually the FICO score, is one the resources lenders use to make lending decisions and to set rates.

CVV. This stands for card verification value. This code is also called the security code. For American Express, the CVV is a four-digit number on the front of the card. For Visa, MasterCard, and Discover cards, the CVV is a three-digit number located on the back of the card.

Default. If you don't pay your credit card bill by the due date, you're in default. This can cause APR increases or you might be given a penalty rate. If your account is seriously delinquent, the credit card issuer can take legal action.

Due date. Your credit card bill has a due date and if you don't pay your bill by that date, you could be charged a late fee and accrue interest charges.

EMV card. This is a credit card that meets the standard for chip-and-PIN cards that are used in Europe. EMV stands for Europe, Master Card, and Visa.

Finance charge. This is the amount of interest you pay when you carry a balance.

Fixed-APR. This is an annual percentage rate that stays the same and does not go up or down with the prime rate.

Foreign transaction fee. These fees are charged on purchases made in a foreign currency or on purchases that involve a foreign bank. These fees usually range from 1 percent to 3 percent. Some credit card companies do not charge these fees. Capital One and Discover don't charge them on any of their cards. The other major issuers waive these fees on certain cards.

"Go-to" rate. This is the interest rate you are charged after your introductory rate ends.

Grace period. The grace period is the time during which you can pay your credit card bill in full and pay no interest charges. They are usually between 20 and 25 days long.

Hard inquiry. This is also referred to as a hard pull. This occurs when you apply for credit and the potential lender reviews your credit report. Each hard inquiry can take two to five points off your FICO score. An exception, though, is when you are rate shopping, such as for a mortgage or auto loan. If you rate shop within a short time frame, the FICO score recognizes this and only counts it as one hard inquiry. Hard inquiries stay on your report for two years, but they're only factored into your FICO score for one year.

Hold. With credit cards (and debit cards, too), a portion of your credit limit might be put on "hold" if the final amount of your transaction is in doubt. For instance, this happens at gas stations and hotels.

Interest rate. This is the cost of borrowing money. With credit cards, the interest rate is usually stated as the APR and so includes the cost of yearly fees.

Introductory APR. This is the APR you get when you open a new account. It is in effect for a specified period of time and, when it ends, your new APR is the go-to rate. Introductory rates are sometimes called teaser rates.

Inquiry. When someone looks at your credit report to decide if you should be approved for credit, they are making an inquiry. A soft inquiry doesn't hurt your score, but a hard inquiry does.

Issuer. This refers to a financial institution that offers, or issues, a credit card. For example, Chase is an issuer, but Visa is not. Rather, Visa is a payment processor.

Joint account. A joint account is a credit card account that is owned by two (or more) people. The parties involved share equal legal liability for the account and any debt.

Late payment fee. This is a fee that is charged if your payment is received after the due date.

Minimum interest charge. This is the minimum amount of interest you will be charged if you are charged any interest.

Minimum payment. If you don't pay your entire balance, this is the lowest amount of money you can pay in a given month.

Opt in. Giving your credit card company or bank permission to include you in a particular service means to opt-in.

Opt out. Declining a particular service or a change in the terms of your credit card contract means to opt- out.

Over-the-limit fee. This refers to a fee that's charged to your account if your balance exceeds your credit limit. You will not be charged this fee unless you have opted in to allow transactions that go over your credit limit.

Penalty APR. This is the APR you'll be charged on new transactions if you do an action that triggers the penalty terms. The terms vary by issuer, but it's usually paying late, exceeding your credit limit, or bouncing a check. These rates can be very high. If you're over 60 days late, the penalty APR could be applied to your entire existing balance.

Piggybacking. People trying to improve their credit scores by becoming an authorized user on someone else's credit card is referred to as piggybacking. The account owner must have excellent credit for this to work.

Preapproved. If you're preapproved for a credit card, it means you passed the initial screening process. You still have to apply and approval isn't guaranteed.

Premium credit card. These credit cards usually have high credit limits, rewards, and excellent benefits and perks.

Prime borrower. A prime borrower has an excellent credit history and gets the lowest rates from credit card issuers.

Prime rate. This is the rate that banks charge their most creditworthy (or prime) customers (usually businesses). Credit card issuers use it as an index to set rates for their customers. Most APRs are variable and they move up and down with the prime rate. APRs are prime plus a margin.

Purchase APR. This is the APR you pay for purchases if you carry a balance on your credit card. If a credit card doesn't have a grace period, this is the rate of interest you start paying when the transaction is posted to your account.

Revolving credit. This refers to a line of credit that doesn't require a specific repayment schedule. Credit cards are revolving credit.

Schumer Box. The Schumer Box is a "box" that discloses the rates and fees for a credit card.

Secured credit card. Secured cards help people with limited or bad credit establish or rebuild a credit history. A deposit is made in an account to "secure" the card. The security deposit usually equals the credit limit, though some cards allow a higher limit than the deposited amount.

Soft inquiry. This is also referred to as a soft pull. As opposed to a hard inquiry, a soft inquiry does not affect your credit score at all. Some examples include checking your own credit reports, credit checks made by companies that want to offer you something, such as a credit card, or credit checks made by a business you already have an account with. Sometimes a potential employer will look at your credit, but unless you've given permission for a hard inquiry, this is also a soft inquiry.

Terms and conditions. Card issuers describe various practices in detail in this part of the disclosure statements. It's considered a legal contract.

Universal default. Before the CARD Act, this was a common practice. Cardholders who failed to make timely payments to other lenders, such as mortgage and car lenders, would see their APRs raised by their credit card issuer, even if they paid their credit card bills on time.

Unsecured credit cards. Unsecured credit cards are not secured by any type of collateral. If you don't pay your bills, issuers can't take your property, for example. This is why you need decent credit and a shown ability to repay debt to get an unsecured card.

Variable-rate APR. This is an APR that goes up and down with the prime rate, unless another index, such as the LIBOR (London Interbank Offered Rate) rate is specified.

Index

Accidental Debtor personality, 68-69, 75

Airline-branded cards, 72, 122, 126

Airport lounge access, 136

Alternative credit, 106-107

AMP Credit Report, 107

Annual fees, 86, 113, 130-131

Annual percentage rate for balance transfers, 83-84

Annual percentage rate for cash advances, 84

Annual percentage rate for purchases, 82-83

Authorized users, 105-106, 181

Auto rental insurance, 117

AwardWallet.com, 140

Balance calculation, 89-90

Balance transfer credit cards, 159-171

Balance transfer fee, 87

Balance transfer nightmares, 166-169

Balance transfers, 83-84, 202-203

Balance transfers, debt and, 186-187

Balances, carrying, 25-26

Banks, 21, 28, 202-203

Banks, social media and, 196-197

Bonus hopping, 187-189

Budget, 23-25

Business credit cards, 73, 143-158

Card verification value, 45

CardHub, 77, 149, 150

CardRatings.com, 77

Carrying balances, 25-26

Cash advance fee, 87

Cash advances, 84

Cash back cards, 122-124

Cash back cards, 71

Charge cards, 73, 122, 127-128

Chip-and-PIN cards, 199-200

Chip-and-signature cards, 199-200

Churning, 189

Co-branded cards, 122, 124-125

College students, 75-76, 96, 99-100

COLLOQUY, 140

Companion certificates, 139

Comparing credit cards, 76-77

Confessions of a Shopaholic, 13, 17

Consumer Financial Protection
Bureau (CFPB), 45, 85, 93, 100

Convenience checks, 162-163

Corporate veil, 144-145

Cosigners, 181

Credit CARD Act of 2009, 36,
    56-60, 76, 84, 85, 87-88,
    89, 98-99, 146-147, 149, 194

Credit card arbitrage, 185-186

Credit card comparison Websites, 77

Credit card personality, 61-78

Credit card trends, 193-203

Credit card types, 70-76

Credit cards, maxing out, 26-28

Credit cards, smartphones and,
    195-196

Credit counselor, 54

Credit crunch, 111

Credit history, length of, 51

Credit Karma, 48, 78

Credit limits, 92

Credit monitoring, 49-50

Credit repair, 174, 151

Credit report, 31, 36, 40-42

Credit report, errors on a, 39, 42

Credit report, free, 40

Credit score, 16, 18, 20, 21, 26-27,
    36, 46, 101, 151, 184

Credit Sesame, 48, 49

Credit utilization ratio, 169,
    178-178

Credit, alternative, 106-107

Credit, new, 52

Credit, rebuilding, 173-182

Credit.com, 48, 49, 77

CreditCards.com, 77

CreditDonkey.com, 77

Debt collectors, 16

Debt, 170-171

Debt, balance transfers and, 186-187

Debt, ignoring, 29-31

Detweiler, Gerri, 194

Diner's Club card, 95

Dispute letter, 42-43

Double-cycle billing, 148

Durbin Amendment, 198

Dynamic Currency Conversion, 141

Earnings, caps on reward, 131-132

eCredable.com, 107

Equal Credit Opportunity Act, 97

Equifax Beacon Score, 47

Equifax, 36-37, 107

Errors on a credit report, 39, 42

Exchange rates, 141

Experian Plus Score Model, 40, 47, 49

Experian, 36-37, 47, 107, 197

Facebook, 196-197

Fair Credit Reporting Act, 38

Federal Deposit Insurance Corporation (FDIC), 93

Federal Reserve, 57, 85, 143, 193

Federal Trade Commission, 39, 42, 85, 174

Fees, 86-88

FICO 08 score, 105-106

FICO score, 27, 35, 40, 45-46, 50-56, 101, 159-160, 176, 178, 183, 188-189

Financial goals, 32

Fine print, 21-22, 79-93, 120, 163-166

Fine print, rewards and, 128-129

Foreign transaction fee, 87, 141

Fraud, 44-45

Free credit report, 40

FreeCreditScore.com, 47

Glyph, 195-196

Goals, financial, 32

Google Wallet, 201

Government Accountability Office, 93

Hard inquiry, 37-38, 177, 188

Hotel-branded cards, 122, 126-127

Identity theft protection, 82

Identity theft, 44-45, 49

Ignoring debt, 29-31

Immigrants, 96

Income level, 54

Installment account, 37

Insurance, payment protection, 92-93

Interest rates, 111-113

Interest, 84-85

Introductory offers, 115-116

Juggler personality, 67-68, 73-74, 109, 111

Late payment fee, 87

Late payments, 28-29

Loss of rewards, 134

LowCards.com, 77

Maxing out credit cards, 26-28

McNamara, Frank, 95

Mindful spending, 24-25

Minimum interest charge, 85

Minimum payments, 90-91

Mintel Comperemedia, 110

Mintel, 193, 196

Mobile wallets, 200-201

Money management help, 119-120

Monitoring, credit, 49

Mortgage Credit Score, 46

Near-field communication
        technology (NFC), 201

Nerdwallet, 77

New credit, 52

Older consumers, 96

Over-the-credit-limit fee, 87-88

Partner programs, rewards and, 139

Payment history, 37, 51

Payment network, 97-98, 102

Payment protection insurance,
        92-93

Payment reminders, 179

Payments, late, 28-29

Payments, minimum, 90-91

Penalty APR, 84

Penalty fees, 87

Personality, credit card, 61-78

Piercing the corporate veil, 144-145

Piggybacking, 105

Point Tracker, 141

Points cards, 72-73

Power User personality, 70-73,
        110, 183-192

Prepaid cards, 103-104, 197-199

Product add-ons, 92

Protection of Young Consumers, 99

Public assistance, 54

Purchases, APR for, 82

Rebuilder personality, 68, 74-75

Rebuilding credit, 173-182

Responsibility, credit cards and,
        11-12

Retail credit cards, 75, 122,
        124-125, 177-178

Returned check fee, 87

Returned payment fee, 87

Revolving account, 37

Reward Summit, 196

Rewards credit cards, 109-120,
        121-131

Rewards padding, 189-191

Rewards programs, 12

Rewards, fine print and, 128-129

Rewards, loss of, 134

Rewards, tracking, 140

Sacrifice, 25

Sallie May, 100

Schneider, Ralph, 95

Schumer Box, 80, 81-88, 91

Schumer, Charles, 80

Secured credit cards, 74, 104-105, 175-177

Sign-up bonuses, 129-130

Small Business Credit Card Study, 149, 150

Smart chip technology, 136

Smartphones, credit cards and, 195-196

Smorecard, 196

Social media, banks and, 196-197

Social media, credit cards and, 110

Soft inquiry, 37

Spending, mindful, 24-25

Store credit cards, 122, 124-125

Store rewards cards, 125

Student cards, 104

T. Rowe Price, 99

Talk Credit Radio Show, 194

Terms, 80-81

Tracking rewards, 140

Tradeline renting, 105

Transaction fees, 86-87

TransUnion TransRisk Score, 47, 48

TransUnion, 36-37, 107

Travel hacking, 187-189

Travel perks, 116-117

Travel rewards cards, 72, 122, 125-126

Trends, credit card, 193-203

Truth in Lending Act, 90

Twitter chats, 197

Types of credit cards, 70-76

U.S. Bureau of Economic Analysis, 193

Unsecured credit cards, 102-103, 106

Utilization ratio, 169, 178-179

VantageScore, 46-47

Visa Signature, 135

Walking Disaster personality, 69-70

Weston, Liz, 193

World MasterCard, 135, 136

Young adults, 96, 98-100

About the Author

Beverly Harzog is a nationally recognized credit card expert, consumer advocate and author. She's appeared on Fox News, ABC News Now, CNN Newsource, and in major media markets, including New York City, Philadelphia, Boston, and San Francisco. She's also a frequent guest on syndicated radio shows across the country, including ABC News Radio.

Her advice can also be found in print and on major Websites, including *The Wall Street Journal*, *CNNMoney.com*, *The New York Times*, *USA Today*, *SmartMoney*, *Money Magazine*, *ABCNews.com*, *NBCNews.com*, *New York Daily News*, *Washington Post*, *Time.com*, *Associated Press*, *MSNMoney.com*, *Reuters.com*, *Inc.*, *Entrepreneur*, *Family Circle*, *Real Simple*, *Bankrate.com*, *CNBC.com*, *Atlanta Journal-Constitution*, *Chicago Tribune*, and more. She's also the credit card columnist for the popular personal finance Website WiseBread.com.

Confessions of a Credit Junkie: Everything You Need to Know to Avoid the Mistakes I Made is her third book. She's also the co-author of *The Complete Idiot's Guide to Person-to-Person Lending* (Alpha Books/Penguin, April 2009) and *Simple Numbers, Straight*

Talk, Big Profits: Four Keys to Unlock Your Business Potential (Greenleaf Publishing, June 2011).

She's a regular speaker at College Week Live, the world's largest on-line college fair, and at national conferences, including the American Society of Journalists and Authors and the Finance Bloggers Conference.

Beverly is a former CPA and has an MBA from the University of New Haven in Connecticut. She also spent two years in a doctoral program at the University of Georgia studying speech communication.

She lives with her husband, two children, an emotionally needy Maltese, and a water snake (no, really) in Johns Creek, Georgia, a northern suburb of Atlanta. She's an exercise junkie, loves to listen to music (everything but country), and is a lifelong Atlanta Braves fan.

You can follow her on Twitter: @BeverlyHarzog. And you can get her expert credit card reviews and the latest buzz on credit cards by visiting her popular credit card blog on her Website, *www.beverlyharzog.com*.